Copyright © 2011 XAMonline, Inc.
All rights reserved. No part of the material protected by this copyright notice may be reproduced or utilized in any form or by any means, electronic or mechanical, including photocopying, recording or by any information storage and retrievable system, without written permission from the copyright holder.

To obtain permission(s) to use the material from this work for any purpose including workshops or seminars, please submit a written request to:

XAMonline, Inc.
25 First Street, Suite 106
Cambridge, MA 02141
Toll Free: 1-800-509-4128
Email: info@xamonline.com
Web: www.xamonline.com
Fax: 1-617-583-5552

Library of Congress Cataloging-in-Publication Data

Wynne, Sharon A.
    ILTS English Language Arts 111 Practice Test 2: Teacher Certification /
Sharon A. Wynne. -1st ed.
    ISBN: 978-1-60787-202-3
    1. ILTS English Language Arts 111 Practice Test 2
    2. Study Guides   3. ILTS   4. Teachers' Certification & Licensure
    5. Careers

Disclaimer:
The opinions expressed in this publication are the sole works of XAMonline and were created independently from the National Education Association, Educational Testing Service, or any State Department of Education, National Evaluation Systems or other testing affiliates.

Between the time of publication and printing, state specific standards as well as testing formats and website information may change that is not included in part or in whole within this product. Sample test questions are developed by XAMonline and reflect similar content as on real tests; however, they are not former tests. XAMonline assembles content that aligns with state standards but makes no claims nor guarantees teacher candidates a passing score. Numerical scores are determined by testing companies such as NES or ETS and then are compared with individual state standards. A passing score varies from state to state.

Printed in the United States of America   œ-1
ILTS English Language Arts 111 Practice Test 2
ISBN: 978-1-60787-202-3

High School English
Post-Test Sample Questions

1. Mark is able to understand the literary text better when he reads it aloud. What is his learning style?
   (Rigorous)

   A. Visual

   B. Verbal

   C. Aural

   D. Physical

2. Ms. Hodnett shows her students an editorial cartoon and asks students to explain the artist's point of view? What skill is she developing in her students?
   (Easy)

   A. Inferencing

   B. Summarizing

   C. Monitoring

   D. Paraphrasing

3. After her class has read through Hamlet's "To be or not to be" soliloquy, Ms. Rook asks them several objective questions about its meaning. What process is she using to help them interpret text?
   (Rigorous)

   A. Inferencing

   B. Summarizing

   C. Monitoring

   D. Paraphrasing

Directions: Read this paragraph and answer questions 4–6.

(1) The drama begins to unfold with the arrival of the corpse at the mortuary.

(2) Alas, poor Yorick! (3) How surprised he would be to see how his counterpart of today is whisked off to a funeral parlor and is in short order sprayed, sliced, pierced, pickled, trussed, trimmed, creamed, waxed, painted, rouged, and neatly dressed-transformed from a common corpse into a Beautiful Memory Picture. (4) This process is known in the trade as embalming and restorative art, and is so universally employed in the United States and Canada that the funeral director does it routinely, without consulting corpse or kin. (5) He regards as eccentric those few who are hardy enough to suggest that it might be dispensed with. (6) Yet no law requires embalming, no religious doctrine commends it, nor is it dictated by considerations of health, sanitation, or even of personal daintiness. (7) In no part of the world but in Northern America is it widely used. (8) The purpose of embalming is to make the corpse presentable for viewing in a suitably costly container; and here too the funeral director routinely, without first consulting the family, prepares the body for public display.
—Jessica Mitford, "Behind the Formaldehyde Curtain"

4. **What is the main idea of this paragraph?**
   (Easy)

   A. Sentence 3

   B. Sentence 4

   C. Sentence 5

   D. Sentence 8

5. **What literary term can be used to define the phrase "Beautiful Memory Picture"?**
   (Average)

   A. Hyperbole

   B. Euphemism

   C. Bathos

   D. Aphorism

6. **What literary term can be used to define the phrase "Alas, Poor Yorick"?**
   (Average)

   A. Conceit

   B. Allusion

   C. Metaphor

   D. Epiphany

7. Which of the following is an effective summary of this paragraph?
(Average)

Resources such as educational software and the Internet expose students to a vast range of experiences and promote interactive learning. Through the Internet, students can communicate with other students anywhere in the world, allowing them to share experiences and viewpoints. Students also use the Internet for individual research projects and to gather information. Computers play a role in other classroom activities as well, from solving math problems to learning English as a second language. Teachers also may use computers to record grades and perform other administrative and clerical duties. They must continually update their skills so that they can instruct and use the latest technology in the classroom.
   —taken from Occupational Outlook Handbook at
http://www.bls.gov/oco/ocos318.htm

A. To teach today's tech-savvy students, teachers must use computers and Internet as part of their pedagogy

B. Computers play an integral role in the education teachers provide

C. The wealth of information on the Internet is a valuable resource for both teachers and students

D. Computers and the Internet are valuable resources

8. Which of the following questions will most effectively help students identify the main idea of this passage?
(Rigorous)

At a time when many thought that sports were too rough for women, Sally Ride became a nationally ranked tennis player who considered turning pro. At a time when opportunities for women were limited, Ride chose to attend college and majored in non-traditional fields, graduating from Stanford University in California in 1973 with degrees in physics and English. This too is remarkable because few women were expected to excel in math and science. Furthermore, she became a rocket scientist in the true sense when she later earned a doctoral degree in astrophysics.

A. Who is the subject of this passage?

B. What is the author's point of view?

C. Is this excerpt informative or analytical?

D. What is the topic sentence?

9. In this excerpt from "The Story of an Hour" by Kate Chopin, what method of interpreting text will help students understand its meaning?
(*Rigorous*)

"She could see in the open square before her house the tops of trees that were all aquiver with the new spring life. The delicious breath of rain was in the air. In the street below a peddler was crying his wares. The notes of a distant song which some one was singing reached her faintly, and countless sparrows were twittering in the eaves.

There were patches of blue sky showing here and there through the clouds that had met and piled one above the other in the west facing her window."

    A. Understanding symbols

    B. Determining the author's context

    C. Generating questions

    D. Summarizing

10. What is the figure of speech that is not used in this example?
(*Rigorous*)

Uneasy lies the head that wears the crown
        —William Shakespeare

    A. Aphorism

    B. Synecdoche

    C. Antithesis

    D. Inversion

11. What figure of speech is used in this example?
(*Rigorous*)

We must learn to live together as brothers or perish together as fools.
        —Martin Luther King, Jr., speech at St. Louis, 1964

    A. Inversion

    B. Synecdoche

    C. Antithesis

    D. Conceit

12. Which of the following is not an apostrophe?
    (Average)

    A. "Frailty, thy name is woman." —William Shakespeare

    B. "Hail, Holy Light, offspring of heaven firstborn!" —John Milton

    C. "O World, I cannot hold thee close enough!" —Edna St. Vincent Millay

    D. "Gather ye rosebuds while ye may…" —Robert Herrick

13. Which of these literary works does not share the coming-of-age motif?
    (Easy)

    A. *Don Quixote*

    B. *Jane Eyre*

    C. *Adventures of Huckleberry Finn*

    D. *David Copperfield*

14. What figure of speech is used in this excerpt?
    (Rigorous)

    I dwell in a lonely house I know / That vanished many a summer ago.
    —Robert Frost, "Ghost House"

    A. Parallelism

    B. Oxymoron

    C. Paradox

    D. Personification

15. Which of the following is not written in iambic pentameter?
    (Rigorous)

    A. "That time of year thou mayst in me behold
       When yellow leaves, or none, or few, do hang
       Upon those boughs which shake against the cold,
       Bare ruined choirs, where late the sweet birds sang."

    B. "But, soft! what light through yonder window breaks?
       It is the east, and Juliet is the sun."

    C. "Something there is that doesn't love a wall,
       That sends the frozen-ground-swell under it"

    D. "And did those feet in ancient time
       Walk upon England's mountains green?
       And was the holy Lamb of God
       On England's pleasant pastures seen?"

16. What figure of speech is in this example from Shakespeare's "Julius Caesar"?
    (Average)

    "Friends, Romans, countrymen, lend me your ears"

    A. Oxymoron

    B. Onomatopoeia

    C. Metonymy

    D. Symbol

17. What is the major literary element in this paragraph?
    (Easy)

    Three witches decide to confront the great Scottish general Macbeth on his victorious return from a war between Scotland and Norway. The Scottish king, Duncan, decides that he will confer the title of the traitorous Cawdor on the heroic Macbeth. Macbeth, and another General called Banquo, happen upon the three witches. The witches predict that he will one day become king. He decides that he will murder Duncan. Macbeth's wife agrees to his plan. He then murders Duncan assisted by his wife who smears the blood of Duncan on the daggers of the sleeping guards. A nobleman called Macduff discovers the body. Macbeth kills the guards insisting that their daggers smeared with Duncan's blood are proof that they committed the murder. The crown passes to Macbeth. More murders ensue and the bloodied ghost of Banquo appears to Macbeth. Lady Macbeth's conscience now begins to torture her and she imagines that she can see her hands covered with blood. She commits suicide. Macduff kills Macbeth and becomes king.

    A. Setting

    B. Character

    C. Plot

    D. Tone

18. What literary element is most noticeable in this excerpt from Jack London's "To Build a Fire"?
    (Easy)

    Day had broken cold and gray, exceedingly cold and gray, when the man turned aside from the main Yukon trail and climbed the high earth-bank, where a dim and little-travelled trail led eastward through the fat spruce timberland.

    A. Character

    B. Setting

    C. Plot

    D. Theme

19. Which of these techniques will help students determine the theme of a story?
    (Average)

    A. Is the author presenting a view of a particular emotion or behavior which the character is experiencing?

    B. Does the title provide a clue to the theme or main idea which the author wishes to present?

    C. Why did the author write this story?

    D. All of the above

20. **What is a story in verse or prose with characters that represent virtues and vices, either literally or figuratively?**
    (Easy)

    A. Epic

    B. Myth

    C. Allegory

    D. Fable

21. **Who is the father of Greek tragedy?**
    (Average)

    A. Aeschylus

    B. Aristotle

    C. Sophocles

    D. Aristophanes

22. **Which of the following is not a characteristic of an epic?**
    (Average)

    A. A long poem, usually of book length, about a serious subject

    B. Characters with superhuman strength, powers, or knowledge

    C. A vast setting over a large geographic area

    D. Told in a familiar, colloquial language style indicative of the culture

23. **Which of the following authors is not considered a short story writer?**
    (Easy)

    A. Edgar Allan Poe

    B. Walt Whitman

    C. Mark Twain

    D. Guy de Maupassant

24. **Which of the following is not a characteristic of a fable?**
    (Average)

    A. A short, simple story

    B. Provides a moral or lesson

    C. Animal characters that speak and act like humans

    D. Has ribald or risqué humor that was meant to appeal to the lower classes

25. **Which of the following is not a characteristic of traditional Greek tragedy?**
    (Easy)

    A. The hero is brought down by his own tragic flaw

    B. The play uses serious poetic language that evokes pity and fear

    C. The play is written in verse

    D. The hero is of high or noble birth

26. **Which type of comedy was used by the Catholic Church in the Middle Ages to attract the common people?**
    (Average)

    A. Comic drama

    B. Melodrama

    C. Farce

    D. Burlesque

27. **What is the order of the dramatic arc?**
    (Average)

    A. Introduction, Characters, Plot, Setting, Climax

    B. Exposition, Rising Action, Climax, Falling Action, Resolution

    C. Exposition, Climax, Falling Action, Resolution, Denouement

    D. Introduction, Rising Action, Climax, Resolution, Denouement

28. **What is the purpose of a sestet in a Petrarchan sonnet?**
    (Rigorous)

    A. It states a problem, asks a question, or expresses an emotion

    B. It introduces the characters and sets the tone

    C. It resolves a problem, answers a question, or responds to an emotion

    D. It sets the mood and rhyme pattern for the rest of the poem

29. Which type of sonnet is exemplified by the following?
    (Rigorous)

    So oft have I invoked thee for my Muse,
    And found such faire assistance in my verse,
    As every Alien pen hath got my use,
    And under thee their poesy disperse.
    Thine eyes, that taught the dumb on high to sing,
    And heavy ignorance aloft to flie,
    Have added feathers to the learned's wing,
    And given grace a double majestie.
    Yet be most proud of that which I compile,
    Whose influence is thine and born of thee,
    In others'works thou dost but mend the style
    And arts with thy sweet graces graced be.
    But thou art all my art, and dost advance
    As high as learning my rude ignorance.

    A. English sonnet

    B. Italian sonnet

    C. Spenserian sonnet

    D. Petrarchan sonnet

30. What is the poetic form of this example?
    (Rigorous)

    These be
    Three silent things:
    The falling snow... the hour
    Before the dawn... the mouth of one
    Just dead.
    —Adeliade Crapsey

    A. Haiku

    B. Cinquain

    C. Limerick

    D. Ballad

31. What is a reference in a literary work to a person, place or thing in history?
    (Easy)

    A. Allusion

    B. Personification

    C. Illusion

    D. Flashback

32. **Which of the following is not a characteristic of a myth?**
    (Average)

    A. Explanations are given for natural phenomena

    B. Ancient heroes overcome the terrors of the unknown

    C. Often based on fact and true events in ancient Greece and Rome

    D. A traditional tale of cultural significance

33. **Which of the following would not be considered a legend?**
    (Average)

    A. Robin Hood stole from the rich and gave to the poor

    B. By pulling a sword out of a stone, young Arthur was shown to be the heir to the throne

    C. In a Word Series game, Babe Ruth pointed to center field, accurately predicting his next hit would be a home run

    D. Texas-born Pecos Bill could ride a tornado like a bronco and used a rattlesnake for a lasso

34. **Which genre of American Literature focuses on a reverence for nature and the interconnectedness of the life cycle?**
    (Rigorous)

    A. Native American Literature

    B. Colonial Literature

    C. Romantic Literature

    D. Realism Literature

35. **Whose writings from early American literature focused on the everyday life and the hardships of New England settlers?**
    (Average)

    A. William Byrd

    B. William Bradford

    C. Anne Bradstreet

    D. Thomas Paine

36. Which of the following is a prime example of neoclassical writing?
    (Average)

    A. "Inaugural Address," a speech by George Washington

    B. "How to Reduce a Great Empire to a Small One," an essay by Benjamin Franklin

    C. "Speech to the Virginia House of Burgesses," a speech by Patrick Henry

    D. "The Declaration of Independence," written primarily by Thomas Jefferson

37. With what literary period are Washington Irving, Nathaniel Hawthorne, and Herman Melville associated?
    (Average)

    A. The Romantic Period

    B. The Realism Period

    C. The Neoclassical Period

    D. The Colonial Period

38. Which of the following is a novel by Nathaniel Hawthorne?
    (Easy)

    A. *Leatherstocking Tales*

    B. *Billy Budd*

    C. *Evangeline*

    D. *The Scarlet Letter*

39. Which essay defined qualities of hard work and intellectual spirit required of Americans in their growing nation?
    (Rigorous)

    A. "The American Scholar" by Ralph Waldo Emerson

    B. "On the Duty of Civil Disobedience" by Henry David Thoreau

    C. "On Walden Pond" by Henry David Thoreau

    D. "Self-Reliance" by Ralph Waldo Emerson

40. Who is the author and what is the subject of this poem?
(Average)

When lilacs last in the door-yard bloom'd,
And the great star early droop'd in the western sky in the night,
I mourn'd—and yet shall mourn with ever-returning spring.

O ever-returning spring! trinity sure to me you bring;
Lilac blooming perennial, and drooping star in the west,
And thought of him I love.

A. Emily Dickinson writing about her secret romance with a local farmer's son

B. Walt Whitman writing about the death of Abraham Lincoln

C. Edgar Allan Poe writing in the persona of a young maiden whose lover has died

D. Henry Wadsworth Longfellow writing about adversity and sorrow in the lives of Native Americans

41. In what way did American Realistic writers differ from American Romantic writers?
(Rigorous)

A. Realistic writers wrote of common, ordinary people and events using details to show the harshness of life while Romantic writers created characters whose will and determination helped them rise above adversity

B. Romantic writers wrote of common, ordinary people and events using details to show the harshness of life while Realistic writers created characters whose will and determination helped them rise above adversity

C. Realistic writers wrote about notable people and events using details to encourage readers to follow their example while Romantic writers wrote about common people and everyday events to warn readers about the depravity of the human soul

D. Romantic writers wrote about notable people and events using details to encourage readers to follow their example while Realistic writers wrote about common people and everyday events to warn readers about the depravity of the human soul

42. **Which of these was written during the Anglo-Saxon Period of British Literature?**
    (Average)

    A. *Samson Agonistes*

    B. *Le Morte d'Arthur*

    C. *Beowulf*

    D. *The Rape of the Lock*

43. **In what period of British literature was this verse written?**
    (Rigorous)

    Lo I the man, whose Muse whilome did maske,
    As time her taught, in lowly Shepheards weeds,
    Am now enforst a far unfitter taske,
    For trumpets sterne to chaunge mine Oaten reeds,
    And sing of Knights and Ladies gentle deeds;
    Whose prayses hauing slept in silence long,
    Me, all too meane, the sacred Muse areeds
    To blazon broad emongst her learned throng:
    Fierce warres and faithfull loues shall moralize my song.

    A. Anglo-Saxon Period

    B. Medieval Period

    C. Renaissance Period

    D. Seventeenth Century

44. **Which of these works of British Literature was not written during the seventeenth century?**
    (Rigorous)

    A. "A Valediction: Forbidding Mourning"

    B. *The Pilgrm's Progress*

    C. *Paradise Lost*

    D. "The Lamb"

45. **What was the preferred writing style of the Enlightenment of the eighteenth century?**
    (Rigorous)

    A. Realism

    B. Romanticism

    C. Naturalism

    D. Neoclassicism

46. In which period of British Literature was this poem written? *(Average)*

    I wandered lonely as a cloud
    That floats on high o'er vales and hills,
    When all at once I saw a crowd,
    A host, of golden daffodils;
    Beside the lake, beneath the trees,
    Fluttering and dancing in the breeze.

    A. The Restoration Period

    B. The Enlightenment Period

    C. The Romantic Period

    D. The Victorian Period

47. Which of these authors did not write during the Victorian Period of British literature? *(Average)*

    A. Gerard Manley Hopkins

    B. Rudyard Kipling

    C. Elizabeth Barrett Browning

    D. Jane Austen

48. Which of the following authors is not from South America? *(Average)*

    A. Gabriela Mistral

    B. Joao Guimaraes Rosa

    C. Jorge Luis Borges

    D. Octavio Paz

49. Which of these is not a Russian novel of psychological realism? *(Average)*

    A. *The Cherry Orchard*

    B. *Crime and Punishment*

    C. *Brothers Karamazov*

    D. *War and Peace*

50. **Which of the following is a characteristic of adolescent literature prior to the twentieth century?**
    (Rigorous)

    A. Adolescent literature was designed to teach history, manners, and morals

    B. Adolescent literature was written to be escapist harmless adventures

    C. Adolescent literature was ignored because so many children were uneducated

    D. Adolescent literature was written only for children of the upper classes

51. **Which of these examples of children's literature was not written in the eighteenth century?**
    (Rigorous)

    A. Daniel Defoe's *Robinson Crusoe*

    B. Jonathan Swift's *Gulliver's Travels*

    C. John Newberry's *A Little Pretty Pocket-Book*

    D. Lewis Carroll's *Alice in Wonderland*

52. **Which of the following characteristics identifies readers at the seventh and eighth grade reading levels?**
    (Rigorous)

    A. Concern with establishing individual and peer group identities

    B. Strong perception of identity

    C. An awareness of ethics required by society

    D. Motivated by peer associations

53. **Which of these works would represent the concept of local color?**
    (Rigorous)

    A. "The Outcast of Poker Flats"

    B. "Daisy Miller: A Study"

    C. *Poems on Various Subjects*

    D. *Walden*

54. **Which period of literature emphasizes the individual, validates emotions and feelings, and looks to nature for inspiration?**
    (Easy)

    A. Neoclassicism

    B. Romanticism

    C. Realism

    D. Naturalism

55. Which of the following is not a member of the second generation of Romantic writers?
(Rigorous)

    A. John Keats

    B. Lord Byron

    C. Ralph Waldo Emerson

    D. Percy Bysshe Shelley

56. Which term can be defined as using all of one's experiences, learning, and development to comprehend information?
(Easy)

    A. Prior knowledge

    B. Context clues

    C. Comprehension

    D. Cues

57. In her journal, Gwenna writes an entry about reading *The Diary of Anne Frank*. Gwenna says that she understood how Anne felt about her mother since she had a fight with her own mother that morning before catching the school bus. What type of reading response does this represent?
(Average)

    A. Critical

    B. Emotional

    C. Interpretive

    D. Evaluative

58. Thom has explicated the Robert Frost poem "Mending Wall" in his final exam by analyzing the way the poem uses imagery and figures of speech to develop the theme of the poem. What type of literary response is this?
(Average)

    A. Emotional

    B. Interpretive

    C. Critical

    D. Evaluative

59. Mr. King has pulled together portfolios of students' work he has graded throughout the year. What is the correct term for this process?
(Rigorous)

    A. Evaluation

    B. Planning

    C. Assessment

    D. Interpretation

60. In Texas, students in the 10th grade participate in a series of tests called the Texas Assessment of Knowledge and Skills. What type of assessment is this?
(Average)

    A. Formal

    B. Informal

    C. Holistic

    D. Summative

61. Which of these is not a skill to be evaluated when assessing reading comprehension?
(Average)

    A. The ability to use schematic cues to connect words with prior knowledge

    B. The ability to use interpretive thinking to make logical predictions and inferences

    C. The ability to use secondary sources to clarify word meaning

    D. The ability to use appreciative thinking to respond to the text, whether emotionally, mentally, or ideologically

62. **Which of the following is not correct?**
    (Rigorous)

    A. Good readers may substitute a word that does not fit the syntax, and will not correct themselves; poor readers will expect the word to fit the syntax they are familiar with.

    B. Good readers will incorporate what they know with what the text says or implies; poor readers may think only of the word they are reading without associating it with prior knowledge

    C. Good readers will apply letter and sound associations almost subconsciously; poor readers may have undeveloped phonics skills or may use phonics skills in isolation

    D. Good readers will consider the meanings of all the known words in the sentence; poor readers may read one word at a time with no regard for the other words

Directions: Read this poem and answer questions 63–66.

Piano

Softly, in the dusk, a woman is singing to me;
Taking me back down the vista of years, till I see
A child sitting under the piano, in the boom of the tingling strings
And pressing the small, poised feet of a mother who smiles as she sings.

In spite of myself, the insidious mastery of song
Betrays me back, till the heart of me weeps to belong
To the old Sunday evenings at home, with winter outside
And hymns in the cosy parlour, the tinkling piano our guide.

So now it is vain for the singer to burst into clamour
With the great black piano appassionato. The glamour
Of childish days is upon me, my manhood is cast
Down in the flood of remembrance, I weep like a child for the past.

—D.H. Lawrence

63. **What type of poetry is "Piano"?**
    (Easy)

    A. Lyric

    B. Dramatic

    C. Narrative

    D. Epic

64. How can students determine the meaning of the word "insidious" used in line 5 of the poem?
(Average)

A. Context clues through word forms

B. Context clues through punctuation

C. Context clues through explanation

D. Context clues through sentence clues

65. How is connotation used to convey meaning in this poem?
(Average)

A. The words "insidious" and "betrays" convey the dark feelings of the poet

B. The end rhyme scheme mimics the beat of the piano

C. The repetition of the word "weep" adds impact

D. The musical term "appassionato" adds authenticity

66. **What would be an effective paraphrase of this poem?** *(Average)*

A. "Piano" is a lyric poem reflecting the thoughts and feelings of a single speaker as he listens at dusk to a woman singing a song that brings back childhood memories of sitting at his mother's feet while she played the piano. It is a short poem of twelve lines divided into three quatrains, rhymed aabb. The poem contains vivid images, and specific and concrete details provide a clear embodiment of his memory.

B. In the evening, a woman is singing for the speaker. This song takes him back to his childhood, and he sees a child sitting under the piano and listening to the sonorous music produced by the piano. In his childhood, his mother used to sit in a comfortable room and sing hymns. As a mischievous child, he used to press her legs but instead of showing her anger, she used to smile at him. When she sings the subtle song, it takes the speaker back to childhood, and his heart starts longing to be with the same piano at the cozy room of his house on Sunday evening. So, now it's vain for the singer to try to woo him and win his heart as the perfect figure of his mother is still in him, and he's driven back to childhood memories and is weeping like a child for the bygone days.

C. The speaker in "Piano" by D. H. Lawrence is proud to be a full grown man, yet he loves remembering his happy childhood; his nostalgic attitude causes him to feel guilty as if he had betrayed his present state of being. Through effective imagery, Lawrence is able (to describe an image) to help the reader understand the speaker's nostalgic attitude. The diction and tone used in this poem reveal the speaker's struggle as his feelings mix between his desire to be a man and his desire to return to his childhood. The syntax and structure of the poem keep the reader in tune with the flow of the poem. In this poem, a man struggles to remain a man while fighting off his memories of the past, which he feels would be uncharacteristic of his present maturity.

D. In a soft voice, a woman is singing to me. She is causing me to remember and look back through the years until I see in my imagination a child sitting under the piano among the noise of the playing strings and touching my mother's small poised feet while she is singing. Despite the fact that I am a man, I am seduced and song overcomes me—it brings me back through in a beguiling way until I weep in my heart to be a part of the old times on Sunday evenings at home when it is winter outside and where we all sat in the comfortable sitting room with the hymns sounding and with the sound of the piano keys as our guide. Now that those days are over, it is pointless for me to come and make a lot of noise along with a great piano piece that is full of passion. I am enveloped by the memories of the days of my childhood and I no longer am acting like a man, but instead I am weeping like a child because I long for the past.

67. **Which of the following would not be an external factor affecting Juan's language development?**
(Rigorous)

    A. Juan celebrates his 8th birthday

    B. Juan has emigrated from Puerto Rico and will begin 5th grade in an American school

    C. Juan is the youngest of four children

    D. Juan visits the library every week for story hour

68. **Which approach of language development is based on the idea that children learn the rules of language structure and apply them through imitation and reinforcement?**
(Easy)

    A. Learning approach

    B. Linguistic approach

    C. Cognitive approach

    D. Sociocognitive approach

69. **Which of the following would be the least effective way to incorporate the sociocognitive approach to learning development in a classroom?**
(Average)

    A. Provide opportunities for students to make oral presentations

    B. Encourage question-and-answer periods to stimulate discussion

    C. Provide instruction on transformational grammar

    D. Provide opportunities for group work

70. **At what level does peer influence strongly affect language?**
(Average)

    A. Pre-school

    B. Elementary school

    C. Middle school

    D. High school

71. **What is the history of a word called?**
    (Easy)

    A. Vernacular

    B. Neologism

    C. Colloquialism

    D. Etymology

72. **Which of the following is a not true about Old English?**
    (Average)

    A. Introduced in Britain during the fifth century

    B. Based on German language of the Angles, Saxons, and the Jutes

    C. Used by Chaucer in *The Canterbury Tales*

    D. Evolved from Indo-European languages through several hundreds of years

73. **Which of the following is a not true about Middle English?**
    (Average)

    A. Developed in England after the Norman Conquest when William the Conqueror invaded from France

    B. Used phonetic spelling and added more inflections

    C. Used by Chaucer in *The Canterbury Tales*

    D. Marked by the Great Vowel Shift when words like "maed" became "made"

74. **Which of the following is not written in Middle English?**
    (Rigorous)

    A. Here begynneth a treatyse how yt hye
    fader of heuen sendeth dethe to so-
    mon euery creature to come and
    gyue counte of theyr liues in
    this worlde and is in maner
    of a morall playe.

    B. Upon an amblere esily she sat,
    Ywympled wel, and on hir heed an hat
    As brood as is a bokeler or a targe;
    A foot-mantel aboute hir hipes large,
    And on hir feet a paire of spores sharpe.

    C. Oft did she heave her napkin to her eyne,
    Which on it had conceited characters,
    Laund'ring the silken figures in the brine
    That seasoned woe had pelleted in tears,
    And often reading what contents it bears;
    As often shrieking undistinguished woe
    In clamours of all size, both high and low.

    D. HIt befel in the dayes of Vther pendragon when he was kynge of all Englond / and so regned that there was a myty duke in Cornewaill that helde warre ageynst hym long tyme.

75. **Which of the following is true about Modern English?**
    (Rigorous)

    A. Regional dialects remain a barrier to clear communication

    B. The addition of new words has slowed since European immigration tapered off in the early 1900s

    C. Technology has expanded English vocabulary

    D. English is easier to learn because of its rules and structure

76. **Why are changes in syntax slow to occur in the English language?**
    (Rigorous)

    A. The English language depends on word order to communicate meaning.

    B. The majority of English words has multiple meanings and can be used as different parts of speech.

    C. The English language depends heavily on inflections which affects syntax.

    D. Pronunciation and spelling make syntax changes more difficult.

77. **Which of the following words does not have a bound morpheme?**
    (Rigorous)

    A. Contract

    B. Explanation

    C. Dog

    D. Words

78. **In the word "conspirator," what does the prefix "con" mean?**
    (Rigorous)

    A. Under

    B. Not

    C. With

    D. Against

79. **Which of the following is true about spelling?**
    (Rigorous)

    A. English spelling is based on the one-sound, one-letter formula

    B. The English alphabet is based on the Greek alphabet with additions by the Romans

    C. The English adopted the Latin-based alphabet with changes from the Greeks and Romans

    D. English spelling became more erratic after the invention of the printing press

80. **Which of the following is a simple sentence?**
    (Average)

    A. Before doing their homework, they had to finish their chores; Megan set the table for dinner while Isaac peeled the potatoes.

    B. After the class was over, the two students packed up their books and headed to the bus.

    C. They talked and they laughed on their way home.

    D. During 5th period English, Megan and Isaac opened their textbooks, turned to p. 35, and began to read the story in their reader.

81. **Which sentence uses subordination to show cause and effect?**
    (Rigorous)

    A. After you review these terms, you should take the practice test.

    B. Although his insurance would have covered the fender bender, Harry decided to pay the garage himself.

    C. The non-profit reached its fundraising goal this year, which was surprising given the state of the economy.

    D. Because writers are seldom satisfied with their first drafts, they frequently revise and edit to craft a more precise message.

82. **Which of the following sentences has a misplaced modifier?**
(Rigorous)

   A. I showed my dog to the veterinarian with the fleas.

   B. Noxious fumes coming from the nearby plant made the office workers sick

   C. Feeling hot, the children took off their sweaters.

   D. The Honda was out of oil and stalled on the road.

83. **Which of the following sentences has an error in parallel structure?**
(Rigorous)

   A. During lunch, they were exchanging notes, studying for the test, and ate their sandwiches.

   B. The office is well-lit and air conditioned.

   C. Students attend class during the fall, winter, and spring, following a calendar that historically accommodated an agricultural society.

   D. As customers, we expect to be treated courteously and promptly.

84. **Choose the sentence with the correct subject-verb agreement.**
(Average)

   A. Dewey, Cheatham, and Howe are the law firm that represents us.

   B. Neither the gym nor the cafeteria is open on the weekend.

   C. Either of the suggestions are acceptable.

   D. An important assignment, along with many resources, was misplaced.

85. Identify the sentence that is capitalized correctly.
    (Easy)

    A. The Gateway Arch in St. Louis is a memorial to Thomas Jefferson's role in opening the west, to the pioneers who helped shape its history, and to Dred Scott who sued for his freedom in the old courthouse.

    B. The Gateway arch in St. Louis is a memorial to Thomas Jefferson's role in opening the West, to the pioneers who helped shape its history, and to Dred Scott who sued for his freedom in the old Courthouse.

    C. The Gateway Arch in St. Louis is a memorial to Thomas Jefferson's role in opening the west, to the pioneers who helped shape its history, and to Dred Scott who sued for his freedom in the Old Courthouse.

    D. The Gateway Arch in St. Louis is a memorial to Thomas Jefferson's role in opening the West, to the pioneers who helped shape its history, and to Dred Scott who sued for his freedom in the Old Courthouse.

86. Which process do most writers use to help them compose more efficiently and effectively?
    (Average)

    A. Step-by-step process

    B. Paraphrasing

    C. Documentation

    D. In-text citations

87. Which of the following is a common prewriting strategy?
    (Easy)

    A. Keep an idea book; write in a daily journal

    B. Brainstorming

    C. Ask the questions who, what, where, when, and why, and how

    D. All of the above

88. What procedure should you follow during the writing stage?
    (Average)

    A. Prepare an outline

    B. Make a list of all ideas connected with your topic

    C. Write freely

    D. Create a visual map on paper to gather ideas.

89. **In what stage of the writing process do writers make changes in sentences, wording, details, and ideas?**
    (Average)

    A. Prewriting

    B. Writing

    C. Revising

    D. Publishing

90. **What is the goal of the publishing process?**
    (Easy)

    A. To have your work displayed on a bulletin board

    B. To have your work read aloud in class

    C. To have your work printed in a literary magazine or school anthology

    D. All of the above

91. **Which of these errors would be caught by a spellchecker?**
    (Average)

    A. Alice went threw the looking glass.

    B. The pep squad won't not be participating.

    C. I attended seminar about effective teaching techniques.

    D. The coach announced the the starting line-up.

92. **Mr. McCutcheon is helping students write their first draft of an argumentative essay and notes that many students are having a hard time with pronoun-antecedent agreement. What would be an effective teaching strategy?**
    (Rigorous)

    A. Develop a three-day grammar workshop to address mechanical problems

    B. Stop the class and provide a brief explanation of the problem and ways to correct

    C. Assign a homework exercise in which students correct sentences with pronoun-antecedent errors

    D. Distribute grammar textbooks and tell students to review the section on pronoun use

93. **When assessing and responding to student writing, which guideline is not summative?**
    (Rigorous)

    A. Reread the writing and note at the end whether the student met the objective of the writing task

    B. Ask students to submit prewriting and rough-draft materials, including all revisions, with their final draft

    C. When reading the draft for the second time, assess it using the standards previously established

    D. Make sure you address the process as well as the product. It is important that students value the learning process as well as the final product

94. **Which of the following suggestions are used for Integrating Language Arts?**
    (Average)

    A. Create writing activities that are relevant to students by having them write and share with real audiences

    B. Use pre-reading activities such as discussion, writing, research, and journals

    C. Use prewriting activities such as reading model essays, researching a topic, interviewing others, and combining sentences

    D. All of the above

95. **What is not an effective step that students should follow when gathering data or information?**
    (Average)

    A. Keep a record of any sources consulted during the research process

    B. Use only direct quotes to avoid plagiarism

    C. Summarize and paraphrase in their own words without the source in front of them

    D. Use key words and synonyms to search for information

96. **When searching online databases for information about the effects of global warming on the polar ice caps, which Boolean operators will generate the highest number of hits?**
    (Rigorous)

    A. "global warming" and "polar ice caps"

    B. "global warming" not "polar ice caps"

    C. "global warming" or "polar ice caps"

    D. (global warming) and (polar ice caps)

97. **What are the two major groups of research materials?**
    (Easy)

    A. Primary and secondary

    B. Hard copy and electronic

    C. Library and online

    D. Informational and analytical

98. **Which of following materials are secondary sources?**
    (Rigorous)

    A. Books written on the basis of primary materials about the period of time

    B. Books written on the basis of primary materials about persons who played a major role in the events under consideration

    C. Books and articles written on the basis of primary materials about the culture, the social norms, the language, and the values of the period

    D. All of the above

99. **Martin is writing a research paper about the role of African Americans in the Vietnam War. Which of these would be an example of primary research?**
    (Rigorous)

    A. Martin reads *Soul Soldiers* by Richard Bailey

    B. Martin finds three online articles about the roles of minorities in the Vietnam War

    C. Martin interviews his grandfather, who served two tours in Vietnam as a medic

    D. Martin finds information on the website www.blackmilitaryworld.com

100. **Which of the following is not an appropriate way to paraphrase correctly?**
    (Average)

    A. Change concept words, special terms, or proper names

    B. Change the key words' form or part of speech

    C. Use synonyms of "relationship words," and use synonyms of phrases and words

    D. Change passive voice to active voice or move phrases and modifiers

101. **Hermione is looking for scholarly information on building an environmentally friendly house. Based on domain names, which site is the most likely to be useful?**
    (Easy)

    A. Wikipedia.com

    B. USA.gov

    C. Greenpeople.org

    D. Healthybuilding.net

102. **What are some the consequences students should be aware of in violating the rules applying to borrowing ideas from various sources?**
    (Average)

    A. Failing an assignment

    B. Expulsion and civil penalties

    C. Losing credit for an entire course

    D. All of the above

103. **Which of the following is the correct example of MLA in-text citation?**
    (Rigorous)

    A. Hu believes that beginning math teachers enter the classroom with a minimal knowledge of math (Hu 2).

    B. Hu believes that beginning math teachers enter the classroom with a minimal knowledge of math (2).

    C. Hu believes that beginning math teachers enter the classroom with a minimal knowledge of math (Hu, 2000).

    D. Hu (2000) believes that beginning math teachers enter the classroom with a minimal knowledge of math (2).

104. **What are the two characteristics that determine language style?**
    (Rigorous)

    A. Degree of formality and word choice

    B. Formal writing and informal writing

    C. Tone and writer's attitude

    D. Point of view and substance

105. Which of the following does not exist in formal language?
    (Rigorous)

    A. Uses shorter sentences and may sound like a conversation

    B. Does not use contractions or slang

    C. Tone - writer's attitude toward the material and/or reader.

    D. Uses longer sentences and does not sound like a conversation

106. Which of the following is not a suggestion that will help students to be more meaningful engaged in their writing?
    (Rigorous)

    A. Write for the teacher as the audience

    B. Write stories that could be read aloud to a group or published in a literary magazine or class anthology

    C. Write for different audiences

    D. Write for different purposes

107. Allyson is preparing a report for the school's English department to recommend a new course for seniors. She determines that of the ten readers, six are women and four are men; eight have bachelor's degrees, one has a master's degree, and one has a doctoral degree. Which of the following has she assessed about her audience?
    (Easy)

    A. Values

    B. Needs

    C. Constraints

    D. Demographics

108. To be convincing, in writing or speaking, which of the following is not one of the three basic principles to follow?
    (Average)

    A. Transition

    B. Coherence

    C. Unity

    D. Emphasis

109. What is the structural problem with this paragraph?
    (Average)

    Club Palm Resort's beaches are beautiful, and the surrounding countryside is quite scenic. The quality of the food leaves a lot to be desired. Many vacationers enjoy the variety of outdoor activities and the instruction available in such sports as sailing and scuba diving. Unfortunately, security is poor; several vacationers' rooms have been broken into and their valuables stolen. Christmas in the Bahamas can make the thought of New Year's in Chicago bearable.

    A. Development

    B. Coherence

    C. Unity

    D. Transition

110. What is a disadvantage of a print message?
    (Easy)

    A. A print message has longevity and is easily portable

    B. A print message requires a skillful reader

    C. A print message appeals to the mind

    D. A print message enables students to re-read sections

111. Which message offers the easiest accessibility for learners?
    (Average)

    A. Print

    B. Audio

    C. Multimedia

    D. Audiovisual

112. What type of written discourse gives information not previously known about a topic or is used to explain or define a topic?
    (Average)

    A. Narrative writing

    B. Descriptive writing

    C. Persuasive writing

    D. Basic expository writing

113. Which of the following provides opportunities for students to apply expository and informative communication?
    (Rigorous)

    A. Speeches

    B. Interviewing

    C. Memorization

    D. Recitation

114. Which of the following would not be an effective delivery technique for oral presentations?
    (Easy)

    A. Maintain a straight but not stiff posture

    B. Refrain from using gestures

    C. Stay within four to eight feet of the front row of your audience

    D. Vary the tone of your voice to show emphasis

115. What uses the idea that facts, statistics, and other forms of evidence can convince an audience to accept a speaker's argument?
    (Rigorous)

    A. Ethos

    B. Pathos

    C. Culture

    D. Logos

116. Which of the following is not a form of inductive reasoning?
    (Average)

    A. Reasoning that goes from general observations to a particular conclusion

    B. Reasoning that goes from particular observations to a general conclusion

    C. Reasoning from a specific case or cases and deriving a general rule

    D. Reasoning that draws inferences from observations in order to make generalizations

117. Which of the following is an example of deductive logic?
    (Rigorous)

    A. All men are mortal; Joe is a man; therefore Joe is mortal

    B. Bachelors are unmarried men; Bill is unmarried; therefore, Bill is a bachelor

    C. A professional basketball game has four periods; we attended a pro basketball game; therefore it had four periods

    D. This cat is black; that cat is black; a third cat is black; therefore all cats are black

118. **What form of persuasive speech appeals to both reason and emotion, and tells listeners what they can do and how to do it?** *(Rigorous)*

    A. Policy

    B. Value

    C. Fact

    D. Argumentation

119. **Which of the following describes third-person omniscient?** *(Easy)*

    A. The narrator is not seen or acting in the story but is able to watch and record not only what is happening or being said but also what characters are thinking

    B. Narrator participates in action but sometimes has limited knowledge/vision

    C. The narrator is all-knowing about one or two characters but not all of them

    D. The narrator talks to the reader and, in essence, draws the reader into the story

120. **In a job interview, Colleen, a recent graduate, explains how proud she is that she worked twenty hours a week while attending college and still maintained a 3.2 GPA. She voices her disdain about other graduates who had no outside jobs and earned lower GPAs. Which form of bias is seen in this example?** *(Rigorous)*

    A. Cultural bias

    B. Racial bias

    C. Professional bias

    D. Unconscious bias

High School English
Post-Test Sample Questions with Rationales

1. **Mark is able to understand the literary text better when he reads it aloud. What is his learning style?**
   (Rigorous)

   A. Visual

   B. Verbal

   C. Aural

   D. Physical

Answer: C. Aural
Because Mark learns better through auditory input, he has an aural learning style. With a visual learning style, a learner understands better through pictures, charts, and video clips. With a verbal learning style, a learner understands through reading and vocabulary. With a physical learning style, a learner has strong kinesthetic skills and would learn better through touch and with manipulatives.

2. **Ms. Hodnett shows her students an editorial cartoon and asks students to explain the artist's point of view? What skill is she developing in her students?**
   (Easy)

   A. Inferencing

   B. Summarizing

   C. Monitoring

   D. Paraphrasing

Answer: A. Inferencing
Inferencing is a process in which the reader makes a reasonable judgment based on the information given. In showing the editorial cartoon and asking for the main idea, the teacher is asking students to use the clues to determine the artist's intent. Summarizing is examining the details of a longer passage or excerpt to determine the main idea. Paraphrasing is a more detailed form of summarizing and follows the chronology of the original piece. Monitoring is a process that students use to stop and think about what they are examining to clarify understanding.

3. After her class has read through Hamlet's "To be or not to be" soliloquy, Ms. Rook asks them several questions about its meaning. What process is she using to help them interpret text?
   (Rigorous)

   A. Inferencing

   B. Summarizing

   C. Monitoring

   D. Paraphrasing

Answer: C. Monitoring
This is monitoring, a process that students use to stop and think about information given. Inference is a process in which the reader makes a reasonable judgment based on the information given. Summarizing is examining the details of a longer passage or excerpt to determine the main idea. Paraphrasing is a more detailed form of summarizing and follows the chronology of the original piece.

Directions: Read this paragraph and answer questions 4–6.

(1) The drama begins to unfold with the arrival of the corpse at the mortuary.

(2) Alas, poor Yorick! (3) How surprised he would be to see how his counterpart of today is whisked off to a funeral parlor and is in short order sprayed, sliced, pierced, pickled, trussed, trimmed, creamed, waxed, painted, rouged, and neatly dressed-transformed from a common corpse into a Beautiful Memory Picture. (4) This process is known in the trade as embalming and restorative art, and is so universally employed in the United States and Canada that the funeral director does it routinely, without consulting corpse or kin. (5) He regards as eccentric those few who are hardy enough to suggest that it might be dispensed with. (6) Yet no law requires embalming, no religious doctrine commends it, nor is it dictated by considerations of health, sanitation, or even of personal daintiness. (7) In no part of the world but in Northern America is it widely used. (8) The purpose of embalming is to make the corpse presentable for viewing in a suitably costly container; and here too the funeral director routinely, without first consulting the family, prepares the body for public display.
—Jessica Mitford, "Behind the Formaldehyde Curtain"

4. What is the main idea of this paragraph?
   (Easy)

   A. Sentence 3

   B. Sentence 4

   C. Sentence 5

   D. Sentence 8

Answer: D. Sentence 8
Sentence 8 is the main idea and works as an effective summary of the paragraph as well. In expository writing, main ideas may appear anywhere in a paragraph and may even be implied.

5. What literary term can be used to define the phrase "Beautiful Memory Picture"?
   (Average)

   A. Hyperbole

   B. Euphemism

   C. Bathos

   D. Aphorism

Answer: D. Aphorism
"Beautiful Memory Picture" is a euphemism for "corpse." A euphemism is the substitution of an agreeable or inoffensive term for one that might offend or suggest something unpleasant. Many euphemisms are used to refer to death, such as "passed away," "crossed over," or nowadays "passed" as a complete reading of this essay will show. Hyperbole is an extreme exaggeration for effect that this phrase borders on. Bathos is a ludicrous attempt to portray pathos—that is, to evoke pity, sympathy, or sorrow. Bathos may result from inappropriately dignifying the commonplace, using elevated language to describe something trivial, or from greatly exaggerated pathos. Aphorism is a focused, succinct expression about life from a sagacious viewpoint.

6. What literary term can be used to define the phrase "Alas, Poor Yorick"? *(Average)*

    A.   Conceit

    B.   Allusion

    C.   Metaphor

    D.   Epiphany

Answer: B. Allusion

"Alas, Poor Yorick" is a line from Act 5 of *Hamlet*, when Hamlet views the skull of his court jester. By using this relevant literary allusion to the topic of her essay, the author sets the tone. A metaphor is an implied comparison. A conceit is an extended metaphor comparing two very dissimilar things (one lofty, one lowly). An epiphany is the moment when something is realized and comprehension sets in.

7. Which of the following is an effective summary of this paragraph?
   (Average)

   Resources such as educational software and the Internet expose students to a vast range of experiences and promote interactive learning. Through the Internet, students can communicate with other students anywhere in the world, allowing them to share experiences and viewpoints. Students also use the Internet for individual research projects and to gather information. Computers play a role in other classroom activities as well, from solving math problems to learning English as a second language. Teachers also may use computers to record grades and perform other administrative and clerical duties. They must continually update their skills so that they can instruct and use the latest technology in the classroom.
   —taken from Occupational Outlook Handbook at
   http://www.bls.gov/oco/ocos318.htm

   A. To teach today's tech-savvy students, teachers must use computers and Internet as part of their pedagogy

   B. Computers play an integral role in the education teachers provide

   C. The wealth of information on the Internet is a valuable resource for both teachers and students

   D. Computers and the Internet are valuable resources

Answer: B. Computers play an integral role in the education teachers provide
A summary is a brief restatement of the main idea. In this paragraph, the main idea of the paragraph is that "Computers play an integral role in the education teachers provide." While the other responses reflect true statements they do not encapsulate the content of the entire paragraph.

8. Which of the following questions will most effectively help students identify the main idea of this passage?
(Rigorous)

At a time when many thought that sports were too rough for women, Sally Ride became a nationally ranked tennis player who considered turning pro. At a time when opportunities for women were limited, Ride chose to attend college and majored in non-traditional fields, graduating from Stanford University in California in 1973 with degrees in physics and English. This too is remarkable because few women were expected to excel in math and science. Furthermore, she became a rocket scientist in the true sense when she later earned a doctoral degree in astrophysics.

- A. Who is the subject of this passage?
- B. What is the author's point of view?
- C. Is this excerpt informative or analytical?
- D. What is the topic sentence?

Answer: B. What is the author's point of view?
By determining the author's point of view, students will be able to determine that the main idea of this paragraph is to discuss the ways in which Sally Ride broke traditional stereotypes and achieved in fields not normally opened for women. Correctly identifying the subject and determining whether the passage is informative or analytical are helpful, but they do not direct the students to the main idea as clearly as the point of view.

9. In this excerpt from "The Story of an Hour" by Kate Chopin, what method of interpreting text will help students understand its meaning?
   (Rigorous)

   She could see in the open square before her house the tops of trees that were all aquiver with the new spring life. The delicious breath of rain was in the air. In the street below a peddler was crying his wares. The notes of a distant song which some one was singing reached her faintly, and countless sparrows were twittering in the eaves.

   There were patches of blue sky showing here and there through the clouds that had met and piled one above the other in the west facing her window."

   A. Understanding symbols

   B. Determining the author's context

   C. Generating questions

   D. Summarizing

Answer: A. Understanding symbols
Understanding symbols can help students determine meaning the author might have intended but not expressed. In most cases, a symbol stands for something that has a deeper meaning than its literal denotation. Symbols can have personal, cultural, or universal associations. In this excerpt, the "open square," "trees...aquiver with the new spring life," "rain," birds singing, "blue sky" and "west" can help students infer more about the character than the author stating an idea directly.

10. What is the figure of speech not used in this example?
    (Rigorous)

    Uneasy lies the head that wears the crown
    —William Shakespeare

    A. Aphorism

    B. Synecdoche

    C. Antithesis

    D. Inversion

Answer: C. Antithesis
This line from Shakespeare's play *King Henry the Fourth* is not an example of antithesis, which is balanced writing about conflicting ideas in sentence form. It does have a synecdoche in the use of the word "head"; synecdoche uses a word for a part of something to mean a whole. It is also an aphorism, which is a short, often witty statement, presenting an observation or a universal truth; an adage. In inversion, the author rearranges the order of words to achieve an effect, such as Yoda in the Star Wars movie "To a dark place this line of thought will carry us" or "Obi-Wan, my choice is." In this example, the subject ("head") and verb ("lies") are inverted.

11. What figure of speech is used in this example?
    (Rigorous)

    We must learn to live together as brothers or perish together as fools.
    —Martin Luther King, Jr., speech at St. Louis, 1964

    A. Inversion

    B. Synecdoche

    C. Antithesis

    D. Conceit

Answer: C. Antithesis
This example uses antithesis because it expresses conflicting ideas in a balanced syntactical structure. Synecdoche uses a part to represent a whole, as in the phrase "all hands on deck." In inversion, the author rearranges the order of words to achieve an effect, such as Yoda in the Star Wars movie "To a dark place this line of thought will carry us" or "Obi-Wan, my choice is." A conceit is an extended metaphor as in the Shakespearean sonnet "Shall I compare thee to a summer day."

12. Which of the following is not an apostrophe?
    (Average)

    A. "Frailty, thy name is woman." —William Shakespeare.

    B. "Hail, Holy Light, offspring of heaven firstborn!" —John Milton.

    C. "O World, I cannot hold thee close enough!" —Edna St. Vincent Millay

    D. "Gather ye rosebuds while ye may…" —Robert Herrick

Answer: D. "Gather ye rosebuds while ye may…" —Robert Herrick
An apostrophe is a literary device of addressing an absent or dead person, an abstract idea, or an inanimate object, as demonstrated in the examples above by Shakespeare, Milton, and Millay. Sonneteers such as Sir Thomas Wyatt, John Keats, and William Wordsworth have addressed the moon, the stars, and the dead Milton. Robert Herrick is talking directly to the reader.

13. Which of these literary works does not share the coming-of-age motif?
    (Easy)

    A. *Don Quixote*

    B. *Jane Eyre*

    C. *Adventures of Huckleberry Finn*

    D. *David Copperfield*

Answer: A. *Don Quixote*
A motif is a key, often repeated phrase, name, or idea in a literary work. The coming-of-age motif is called a *bildungsroman* and is evident in the novels *David Copperfield*, *Jane Eyre*, and *Adventures of Huckleberry Finn*. Cervantes' *Don Quixote* is a novel with a quest motif.

14. What figure of speech is used in this excerpt?
    (Rigorous)

    I dwell in a lonely house I know / That vanished many a summer ago.
    —Robert Frost, "Ghost House"

    A. Parallelism

    B. Oxymoron

    C. Paradox

    D. Personification

Answer: C. Paradox
This excerpt is an example of a paradox, a seemingly untrue statement deliberately employed for effect. Frost writes of living in a house that has disappeared. Similar to paradox, an oxymoron is a contradiction of terms, but it is usually a short phrase as in "hot ice" or "pretty ugly." Parallelism is the arrangement of ideas in phrases, sentences, and paragraphs that balance one element with another of equal importance and similar wording as in Lincoln's "of the people, by the people, and for the people." Personification is giving human characteristics to things or abstract ideas, as in Frost's lines from "Spring Pool": "And like the flowers beside them chill and shiver, Will like the flowers beside them soon be gone."

15. Which of the following is not written in iambic pentameter?
(Rigorous)

A. "That time of year thou mayst in me behold
When yellow leaves, or none, or few, do hang
Upon those boughs which shake against the cold,
Bare ruined choirs, where late the sweet birds sang."

B. "But, soft! what light through yonder window breaks?
It is the east, and Juliet is the sun."

C. "Something there is that doesn't love a wall,
That sends the frozen-ground-swell under it"

D. "And did those feet in ancient time
Walk upon England's mountains green?
And was the holy Lamb of God
On England's pleasant pastures seen?"

**Answer: D. "And did those feet in ancient time
Walk upon England's mountains green?
And was the holy Lamb of God
On England's pleasant pastures seen?"**

Choice D is an excerpt from William Blake's introduction to "Milton" and is written in iambic tetrameter. In poetry, the most common foot or measure is the iamb, which is a pair of syllables; the first syllable is unaccented, and the second syllable is accented. Tetrameter has four feet per line; pentameter has five feet per line. Choice A is the opening lines from Shakespeare's "Sonnet 73." Choice B is from Shakespeare's play *Romeo and Juliet*. Choice C is from Robert Frost's poem "Mending Wall."

16. **What figure of speech is in this example from Shakespeare's "Julius Caesar"?**
    (Average)

    Friends, Romans, countrymen, lend me your ears

    A.   Oxymoron

    B.   Onomatopoeia

    C.   Metonymy

    D.   Symbol

Answer: C. Metonymy
"Lend me your ears" is an example of metonymy, when an object or idea is closely associated with another of which it is associated. Marc Antony was asking the citizens to listen to him and "ears" became the object to associate with listening. Oxymoron is a seemingly contradiction of terms as in the "living dead." Onomatopoeia is the naming of a thing or action by the sound it makes, as when bacon sizzles. A symbol is an object or action that suggests something else as when the color black symbolizes death or the heart symbolizes love.

17. What is the major literary element in this paragraph?
    (Easy)

    Three witches decide to confront the great Scottish general Macbeth on his victorious return from a war between Scotland and Norway. The Scottish king, Duncan, decides that he will confer the title of the traitorous Cawdor on the heroic Macbeth. Macbeth, and another General called Banquo, happen upon the three witches. The witches predict that he will one day become king. He decides that he will murder Duncan. Macbeth's wife agrees to his plan. He then murders Duncan assisted by his wife who smears the blood of Duncan on the daggers of the sleeping guards. A nobleman called Macduff discovers the body. Macbeth kills the guards insisting that their daggers smeared with Duncan's blood are proof that they committed the murder. The crown passes to Macbeth. More murders ensue and the bloodied ghost of Banquo appears to Macbeth. Lady Macbeth's conscience now begins to torture her and she imagines that she can see her hands covered with blood. She commits suicide. Macduff kills Macbeth and becomes king.

    A. Setting

    B. Character

    C. Plot

    D. Tone

Answer: C. Plot
This brief plot summary introduces the characters, setting, and resolution of the story Shakespeare's *Macbeth*.

18. **What literary element is most noticeable in this excerpt from Jack London's "To Build a Fire"?**
(Easy)

Day had broken cold and gray, exceedingly cold and gray, when the man turned aside from the main Yukon trail and climbed the high earth-bank, where a dim and little-travelled trail led eastward through the fat spruce timberland.

    A.   Character

    B.   Setting

    C.   Plot

    D.   Theme

Answer: B. Setting
Jack London establishes the time of day, place, and physical details with a single sentence so that the reader can infer that it is a bleak morning. Character would be the person in the story. Plot is the sequence of events. Theme is the main idea of the story.

19. **Which of these techniques will help students determine the theme of a story?**
(Average)

    A.   Is the author presenting a view of a particular emotion or behavior which the character is experiencing?

    B.   Does the title provide a clue to the theme or main idea which the author wishes to present?

    C.   Why did the author write this story?

    D.   All of the above

Answer: D. All of the above
Theme is the underlying main idea of a piece of literature. It is the controlling idea that the plot, characters, setting, and mood develop. All of these questions will help students determine the theme of a story.

20. **What is a story in verse or prose with characters that represent virtues and vices, either literally or figuratively?**
    (Easy)

    A. Epic

    B. Myth

    C. Allegory

    D. Fable

Answer: C. Allegory
An allegory is a story in verse or prose with characters that represent virtues and vices. Examples of allegories include *The Inferno*, where Dante represents everyone who seeks to understand his purpose in life. Virgil, as his guide, represents reason and wisdom. An epic is a long poem reflecting values in a society. A myth is a story within a culture to explain its history and traditions. A fable is a short tale with a moral.

21. **Who is the father of Greek tragedy?**
    (Average)

    A. Aeschylus

    B. Aristotle

    C. Sophocles

    D. Aristophane

Answer: A. Aeschylus
Aeschylus is known as the father of Greek tragedy, writing almost 90 plays. Aristotle, a student of Plato, was a philosopher and wrote the *Poetics*, which addressed the elements of poetry. Sophocles, another Greek dramatist, wrote almost 120 plays, including the famous *Oedipus* trilogy. While Sophocles is noted for tragedy, Aristophanes is famous for his comedies, such as *Lysistrata*.

22. **Which of the following is not a characteristic of an epic?**
    (Average)

    A. A long poem, usually of book length, about a serious subject

    B. Characters with superhuman strength, powers, or knowledge

    C. A vast setting over a large geographic area

    D. Told in a familiar, colloquial language style indicative of the culture

Answer: D. Told in a familiar, colloquial language style indicative of the culture
The language of an epic is usually elevated speech befitting a long narrative on a serious subject with a wide cast of noble or important characters. *Beowulf*, for example, is a classic epic with a noble character who overcomes monsters. It dates back to the Anglo-Saxon era and is written in Old English.

23. **Which of the following authors is not considered a short story writer?**
    (Easy)

    A. Edgar Allan Poe

    B. Walt Whitman

    C. Mark Twain

    D. Guy de Maupassant

Answer: B. Walt Whitman
Walt Whitman was a nineteenth-century poet, essayist, and journalist, but he is not known for his short stories. Edgar Allan Poe, a nineteenth-century poet, literary critic, and short story writer, is known for his horror stories and is also credited as being the father of the detective story. Guy de Maupassant is a nineteenth-century short story writer, whose "The Necklace" is popularly anthologized. Mark Twain, another nineteenth-century writer, wrote novels and short stories from the comic "The Celebrated Jumping Frog of Calaveras County" to the cynical "The Man That Corrupted Hadleyburg."

24. Which of the following is not a characteristic of a fable?
    (Average)

    A.   A short, simple story

    B.   Provides a moral or lesson

    C.   Animal characters that speak and act like humans

    D.   Has ribald or risqué humor that was meant to appeal to the lower classes

Answer: D. Has ribald or risqué humor that was meant to appeal to the lower classes
Fables can trace their origins to Aesop, the Greek writer of the sixth center BCE. They are brief stories using animals or objects to depict human foibles. They end with a lesson, sometimes called a moral exemplum. They are not necessarily ribald or humorous, although a French variation, the *fabliau*, did include trickery, practical jokes and other types of low humor.

25. Which of the following is not a characteristic of traditional Greek tragedy?
    (Easy)

    A.   The hero is brought down by his own tragic flaw

    B.   The play uses serious poetic language that evokes pity and fear

    C.   The play is written in verse

    D.   The hero is of high or noble birth

Answer: C. The play is written in verse
Traditional Greek tragedy, as established by Aristotle's *Poetics,* can be written in either prose or poetry.

26. **Which type of comedy was used by the Catholic Church in the Middle Ages to attract the common people?**
    (Average)

    A. Comic drama

    B. Melodrama

    C. Farce

    D. Burlesque

Answer: A. Comic drama
Comic drama, with its serious and light elements, originated in the Middle Ages under the auspices of the Catholic Church, which tried to reach the common people via mystery and morality plays. The modern equivalent would be television's "dramedies," which present a serious plot with comic elements. Melodrama has a formulaic structure as in the silent film series the *Perils of Pauline.* Farce is noted for its low humor and physical comedy. Burlesque comedy is another example of low comedy; it began in nineteenth-century America as theatrical entertainment marked by parody but later devolved into striptease shows.

27. **What is the order of the dramatic arc?**
    (Average)

    A. Introduction, Characters, Plot, Setting, Climax

    B. Exposition, Rising Action, Climax, Falling Action, Resolution

    C. Exposition, Climax, Falling Action, Resolution, Denouement

    D. Introduction, Rising Action, Climax, Resolution, Denouement

Answer: B. Exposition, Rising Action, Climax, Falling Action, Resolution
The narrative arc begins with the exposition, which could the introduction of characters and setting. The rising action occurs with the first conflict between the protagonist and antagonist. This builds until the plot reaches the climax, a turning point and the highest peak of action. Following this is the falling action, which can be quite brief. The resolution of the conflict, or denouement, is at the end of the story.

28. **What is the purpose of a sestet in a Petrarchan sonnet?**
(Rigorous)

   A. It states a problem, asks a question, or expresses an emotion

   B. It introduces the characters and sets the tone

   C. It resolves a problem, answers a question, or responds to an emotion

   D. It sets the mood and rhyme pattern for the rest of the poem

Answer: C. It resolves a problem, answers a question, or responds to an emotion
The Petrarchan sonnet generally has a two-part theme. The first eight lines, called the octave, state a problem, ask a question, or express an emotional tension. The last six lines, called the sestet, resolve the problem, answer the question, or relieve the tension. The rhyme scheme of the octave is abbaabba; that of the sestet varies.

29. Which type of sonnet is exemplified by the following?
    (Rigorous)

    So oft have I invoked thee for my Muse,
    And found such faire assistance in my verse,
    As every Alien pen hath got my use,
    And under thee their poesy disperse.
    Thine eyes, that taught the dumb on high to sing,
    And heavy ignorance aloft to flie,
    Have added feathers to the learned's wing,
    And given grace a double majestie.
    Yet be most proud of that which I compile,
    Whose influence is thine and born of thee,
    In others'works thou dost but mend the style
    And arts with thy sweet graces graced be.
    But thou art all my art, and dost advance
    As high as learning my rude ignorance.

    A. English sonnet

    B. Italian sonnet

    C. Spenserian sonnet

    D. Petrarchan sonnet

Answer: A. English sonnet
This is Shakespeare's "Sonnet 78." The English sonnet has three quatrains with independent rhyme schemes followed by a rhyming couplet. The rhyme scheme of this Shakespearean sonnet is ababcdcdefefgg. The Spenserian sonnet follows the English quatrain-and-couplet pattern but resembles the Italian sonnet in its rhyme scheme, which is linked: abab bcbc cdcd ee. The Italian/Petrarchan sonnet has an octave with a abbaabba rhyme scheme and a sestet with a variable rhyme scheme.

30. **What is the poetic form of this example?**
    (Rigorous)

    These be
    Three silent things:
    The falling snow... the hour
    Before the dawn... the mouth of one
    Just dead.

    —Adeliade Crapsey

    A.   Haiku

    B.   Cinquain

    C.   Limerick

    D.   Ballad

Answer: B. Cinquain
A cinquain is a five-line poem with 22 syllables in a set pattern: line 1, two syllables; line 2, four syllables; line 3, six syllables; line 4, eight syllables; line 5, two syllables. It was devised by Adelaide Crapsey and memorialized by Carl Sandburg in a poem about her short life. A haiku is a three-lined poem of five, seven, and five syllables. A limerick is five-lined poem with an aabba rhyme scheme and a set meter within each line. A ballad is a story told in poetic form and was originally intended to be sung. Like music, it will have refrains or repeated sections.

31. **What is a reference in a literary work to a person, place or thing in history?**
    (Easy)

    A. Allusion

    B. Personification

    C. Illusion

    D. Flashback

Answer: A. Allusion
An allusion is a reference in a literary work to a person, place, or thing in history. An example would be in *The Inferno* when Dante alludes to Phaethon and Icarus, both Greek mythological features. By doing so, Dante draws an analogy between their situation and his: fear of the unknown. Personification is giving human characteristics to an inanimate object, an abstract quality, or an animal, as when "the tree sings." Illusion is not a literary term but often a misspelling of allusion; it means a false perception or belief. A flashback is an interruption in the telling of a story to look at past events or an earlier occurrence.

32. **Which of the following is not a characteristic of a myth?**
    (Average)

    A. Explanations are given for natural phenomena

    B. Ancient heroes overcome the terrors of the unknown

    C. Often based on fact and true events in ancient Greece and Rome

    D. A traditional tale of cultural significance

Answer: C. Often based on fact and true events in ancient Greece and Rome
While myths may have some historical authenticity, they are not often based on fact and true events. They often deal with gods, supernatural beings, or ancestral heroes.

33. Which of the following would not be considered a legend?
    (Average)

    A.   Robin Hood stole from the rich and gave to the poor

    B.   By pulling a sword out of a stone, young Arthur was shown to be the heir to the throne

    C.   In a Word Series game, Babe Ruth pointed to center field, accurately predicting his next hit would be a home run

    D.   Texas-born Pecos Bill could ride a tornado like a bronco and used a rattlesnake for a lasso

Answer: D. Texas-born Pecos Bill could ride a tornado like a bronco and used a rattlesnake for a lasso
A legend is a tale based on a real person that is part fact and part fiction. Arthur, Babe Ruth, and Robin Hood were real people whose accomplishments have been exaggerated. Pecos Bill is an imaginary character, and his story is considered a tall tale, a humorously exaggerated tale about impossible events.

34. Which genre of American Literature focuses on a reverence for nature and the interconnectedness of the life cycle?
    (Rigorous)

    A.   Native American Literature

    B.   Colonial Literature

    C.   Romantic Literature

    D.   Realism Literature

Answer: A. Native American Literature
Characteristics of Native American literature include reverence for and awe of nature and the interconnectedness of the elements in the life cycle. Its themes include the hardiness of the native body and soul, remorse for the destruction of the native way of life, and the genocide of many tribes by the encroaching settlement and Manifest Destiny policies of the U.S. government. Colonial literature was neoclassical and emphasized order, balance, clarity, and reason; it had strong ties to British literature at the time. Romantic literature emphasized the individual. Emotions and feelings were validated, and nature acted as an inspiration for creativity. Romantics hearkened back to medieval, chivalric themes and ambiance. The Realists wrote about the common man and his socioeconomic problems in a non-sentimental way.

35. **Whose writings from early American literature focused on the everyday life and the hardships of New England settlers?**
    (Average)

    A.   William Byrd

    B.   William Bradford

    C.   Anne Bradstreet

    D.   Thomas Paine

Answer: C. Anne Bradstreet
Anne Bradstreet's poetry describes colonial New England life. From her journals, modern readers learn about the everyday life of the early settlers, the hardships of travel, and the responsibilities of different groups and individuals in the community. William Bradford's excerpts from *The Mayflower Compact* relate vividly the hardships of crossing the Atlantic in a tiny vessel, the misery and suffering of the first winter, the approaches of the American Indians, the decimation of the colonists' ranks, and the establishment of the Bay Colony of Massachusetts. William Byrd's journal *A History of the Dividing Line,* concerning his trek into the Dismal Swamp separating the Carolinian territories from Virginia and Maryland makes quite lively reading. Thomas Paine's pamphlet *Common Sense* spoke to the American patriots' common sense in dealing with issues in the cause of freedom; this word is considered part of the Revolutionary Period.

36. **Which of the following is a prime example of neoclassical writing?**
    (Average)

    A.   "Inaugural Address," a speech by George Washington

    B.   "How to Reduce a Great Empire to a Small One," an essay by Benjamin Franklin

    C.   "Speech to the Virginia House of Burgesses," a speech by Patrick Henry

    D.   "The Declaration of Independence," written primarily by Thomas Jefferson

Answer: D. "The Declaration of Independence," written primarily by Thomas Jefferson
"The Declaration of Independence," the brainchild predominantly of Thomas Jefferson (along with some prudent editing by Ben Franklin), is a prime example of neoclassical writing—balanced, well crafted, and focused.

37. **With what literary period are Washington Irving, Nathaniel Hawthorne, and Herman Melville associated?**
    (Average)

    A. The Romantic Period

    B. The Realism Period

    C. The Neoclassical Period

    D. The Colonial Period

Answer: A. The Romantic Period
These authors are associated with the Romantic Period of American Literature, which is marked by a distinctly American style of writing devoid of English influences. Washington Irving's characters are distinctly from American folklore. Nathaniel Hawthorne and Herman Melville are the preeminent early American novelists, writing on subjects definitely regional, specific, and American, yet sharing insights about human foibles, fears, loves, doubts, and triumphs.

38. **Which of the following is a novel by Nathaniel Hawthorne?**
    (Easy)

    A. *Leatherstocking Tales*

    B. *Billy Budd*

    C. *Evangeline*

    D. *The Scarlet Letter*

Answer: D. *The Scarlet Letter*
Hawthorne's masterpiece *The Scarlet Letter* criticizes the society of hypocritical Puritan New Englanders, who ostensibly left England to establish religious freedom but who became entrenched in judgmental finger wagging. The Puritans in the novel ostracize Hester Prynne and condemn her child, Pearl, as a child of Satan. Great love, sacrifice, loyalty, suffering, and related epiphanies add universality to this tale. James Fenimore Cooper wrote *Leatherstocking Tales*, Herman Melville wrote *Billy Budd*, and Henry Wadsworth Longfellow wrote the epic poem *Evangeline*.

39. **Which essay defined qualities of hard work and intellectual spirit required of Americans in their growing nation?**
(Rigorous)

   A.   "The American Scholar" by Ralph Waldo Emerson

   B.   "On the Duty of Civil Disobedience" by Henry David Thoreau

   C.   "On Walden Pond" by Henry David Thoreau

   D.   "Self-Reliance" by Ralph Waldo Emerson

Answer: A. "The American Scholar" by Ralph Waldo Emerson
Ralph Waldo Emerson defined the qualities of hard work and intellectual spirit required of Americans in their growing nation in a speech to Thoreau's Harvard graduating class. Emerson also wrote "Self-Reliance," which details his philosophy on individualist. Thoreau wrote passionately regarding his objections to the interference of government in the life of the individual in "On the Duty of Civil Disobedience. Thoreau, who wanted to get to the marrow of life, immersed himself in nature at Walden Pond and wrote an inspiring autobiographical account of his sojourn, aptly titled *On Walden Pond*

40. Who is the author and what is the subject of this poem?
(Average)

When lilacs last in the door-yard bloom'd,
And the great star early droop'd in the western sky in the night,
I mourn'd—and yet shall mourn with ever-returning spring.

O ever-returning spring! trinity sure to me you bring;
Lilac blooming perennial, and drooping star in the west,
And thought of him I love.

- A. Emily Dickinson writing about her secret romance with a local farmer's son

- B. Walt Whitman writing about the death of Abraham Lincoln

- C. Edgar Allan Poe writing in the persona of a young maiden whose lover has died

- D. Henry Wadsworth Longfellow writing about adversity and sorrow in the lives of Native Americans

Answer: B. Walt Whitman writing about the death of Abraham Lincoln
The Civil War period ushered in the poignant poetry of Walt Whitman and his homage to all who suffered from the ripple effects of war and presidential assassination. He wrote "When Lilacs Last in the Courtyard Bloom'd" about the effects of Abraham Lincoln's death on the poet and the nation.

41. In what way did American Realistic writers differ from American Romantic writers?
(Rigorous)

    A.   Realistic writers wrote of common, ordinary people and events using details to show the harshness of life while Romantic writers created characters whose will and determination helped them rise above adversity

    B.   Romantic writers wrote of common, ordinary people and events using details to show the harshness of life while Realistic writers created characters whose will and determination helped them rise above adversity

    C.   Realistic writers wrote about notable people and events using details to encourage readers to follow their example while Romantic writers wrote about common people and everyday events to warn readers about the depravity of the human soul

    D.   Romantic writers wrote about notable people and events using details to encourage readers to follow their example while Realistic writers wrote about common people and everyday events to warn readers about the depravity of the human soul

Answer: A. Realistic writers wrote of common, ordinary people and events using details to show the harshness of life while Romantic writers created characters whose will and determination helped them rise above adversity

Realistic writers wrote of common, ordinary people and events using details to show the harshness of life. An example would be Upton Sinclair's *The Jungle*, which described the deplorable working conditions in Chicago's meatpacking plants. Romantic writers created characters whose will and determination helped them rise above adversity. An example would be James Fenimore Cooper's *Leatherstocking Tales*.

42. Which of these was written during the Anglo-Saxon Period of British Literature?
(Average)

- A. *Samson Agonistes*

- B. *Le Morte d'Arthur*

- C. *Beowulf*

- D. *The Rape of the Lock*

Answer: C. *Beowulf*

Beowulf was anonymously written by Christian monks during the Anglo-Saxon Period, many years after the events in the narrative supposedly occurred. This Teutonic saga relates the triumph over monsters by the hero, Beowulf. The Anglo-Saxon period spanned six centuries and ended with the Norman Conquest in 1066. Thomas Malory's *Le Morte d'Arthur,* written during the Medieval Period of British Literature, brought together extant tales from Europe concerning the legendary King Arthur, Merlin, Guinevere, and the Knights of the Round Table. John Milton wrote the social commentary *Samson Agonistes* in the seventeenth century. Alexander Pope wrote *The Rape of the Lock*, a mock epic, in the eighteenth century.

43. **In what period of British literature was this verse written?**
    (Rigorous)

    Lo I the man, whose Muse whilome did maske,
    As time her taught, in lowly Shepheards weeds,
    Am now enforst a far unfitter taske,
    For trumpets sterne to chaunge mine Oaten reeds,
    And sing of Knights and Ladies gentle deeds;
    Whose prayses hauing slept in silence long,
    Me, all too meane, the sacred Muse areeds
    To blazon broad emongst her learned throng:
    Fierce warres and faithfull loues shall moralize my song.

    A.   Anglo-Saxon Period

    B.   Medieval Period

    C.   Renaissance Period

    D.   Seventeenth Century

Answer: C. Renaissance Period
Written by Edmund Spenser during the Renaissance Period, these eight lines of verse are taken from his epic *The Faerie Queen.* He created a nine-line stanza—eight lines iambic pentameter and an extra-footed ninth line—called an *alexandrine*.

44. **Which of these works of British Literature was not written during the seventeenth century?**
    (Rigorous)

    A.   "A Valediction: Forbidding Mourning"

    B.   *The Pilgrm's Progress*

    C.   *Paradise Lost*

    D.   "The Lamb"

Answer: D. "The Lamb"
"The Lamb" is a poem written by William Blake in the eighteenth century. John Donne wrote the poem "A Valediction: Forbidding Mourning" in 1622 to comfort his wife while he was away on business. John Bunyan wrote the allegory *The Pilgrim's Progress* in 1678 about man's journey to the Celestial City (Heaven). John Milton wrote his religious masterpiece, *Paradise Lost*, around 1650–1660.

45. **What was the preferred writing style of the Enlightenment of the eighteenth century?**
    (Rigorous)

    A. Realism

    B. Romanticism

    C. Naturalism

    D. Neoclassicism

Answer: D. Neoclassicism
During the eighteenth century, neoclassicism became the preferred writing style, especially for Alexander Pope, who strove for metrical correctness in his poetry. The neoclassical style emphasized order and structure. Like the Greeks and Romans, the writers of the Enlightenment dealt with lofty ideas, such as truth and love.

46. **In which period of British Literature was this poem written?**
    (Average)

    **I wandered lonely as a cloud
    That floats on high o'er vales and hills,
    When all at once I saw a crowd,
    A host, of golden daffodils;
    Beside the lake, beneath the trees,
    Fluttering and dancing in the breeze.**

    A. The Restoration Period

    B. The Enlightenment Period

    C. The Romantic Period

    D. The Victorian Period

Answer: C. The Romantic Period
This excerpt, taken from William Wordsworth's poem "Daffodils," written in 1804, exemplifies the writing style of the Romantic Period. It describes an aesthetic experience with picture-like detail. Poets of this period favored imagination over reason and looked to nature for inspiration.

47. Which of these authors did not write during the Victorian Period of British literature?
(Average)

   A.   Gerard Manley Hopkins

   B.   Rudyard Kipling

   C.   Elizabeth Barrett Browning

   D.   Jane Austen

Answer: D. Jane Austen
Like the Bronte sisters, Jane Austen is a novelist of the Romantic Period of British Literature who wrote in the eighteenth century. The other three authors represent the diversity of the Victorian Period of the nineteenth century. Gerard Manley Hopkins, a Catholic priest, wrote poetry using sprung rhythm. Rudyard Kipling wrote about Colonialism in India in works such as *Kim* and *The Jungle Book*, which recreate exotic locales and dissect the Raj, the British Colonial government during Queen Victoria's reign. Elizabeth Barrett Browning wrote two major works, the epic feminist poem *Aurora Leigh* and the deeply moving and provocative *Sonnets from the Portuguese*, in which she details her deep love for Robert Browning.

48. Which of the following authors is not from South America?
(Average)

   A.   Gabriela Mistral

   B.   Joao Guimaraes Rosa

   C.   Jorge Luis Borges

   D.   Octavio Paz

Answer: D. Octavio Paz
North American literature is divided among the United States, Canada, and Mexico. Octavio Paz, author of *The Labyrinth of Solitude*, is a 1990 Nobel Prize–winning poet from Mexico. Chilean Gabriela Mistral was the first Latin American writer to win the Nobel Prize in Literature. She is best known for her collection of poetry, *Desolation and Feeling*. Argentine Jorge Luis Borges is considered by many literary critics to be the most important writer of his century from South America. His collection of short stories, *Ficciones*, brought him universal recognition. Brazil's Joao Guimaraes Rosa wrote the novel *The Devil to Pay*, considered by many to be first-rank world literature

49. **Which of these is not a Russian novel of psychological realism?**
    (Average)

    A. *The Cherry Orchard*

    B. *Crime and Punishment*

    C. *Brothers Karamazov*

    D. *War and Peace*

Answer: A *The Cherry Orchard*
Produced in 1904, *The Cherry Orchard* is the last play written by Anton Chekhov. Although he intended it to be a comedy, the story of an aristocratic family about to lose their estate, has often been produced as a tragedy. *Crime and Punishment* by Fyodor Dostoyevsky is a psychological study of a troubled ex-student who plots and executes a pawnbroker. The novel was first published as monthly installments in 1866. Dostoyevsky's last novel *The Brothers Karamazov*, completed in 1880, focuses on three brothers pondering moral and ethical issues after the murder of their father. Called the national novel of Russia, Leo Tolstoy's *War and Peace* (1869) is a sweeping account in graphic detail of the invasion of Russia and Napoleon's taking of Moscow.

50. **Which of the following is a characteristic of adolescent literature prior to the twentieth century?**
    (Rigorous)

    A. Adolescent literature was designed to teach history, manners, and morals

    B. Adolescent literature was written to be escapist harmless adventures

    C. Adolescent literature was ignored because so many children were uneducated

    D. Adolescent literature was written only for children of the upper classes

Answer: A. Adolescent literature was designed to teach history, manners, and morals
Prior to twentieth-century research on childhood and adolescent development, books for adolescents were primarily didactic. They were designed to address history, manners, and morals. As early as the eleventh century, Anselm, the Archbishop of Canterbury, wrote an encyclopedia designed to instill in children the beliefs and principles of conduct acceptable to adults in medieval society. Fifteenth-century hornbooks were designed to teach reading and religious lessons. In Puritan America, the *New England Primer* set forth the prayers, catechisms, Bible verses, and illustrations meant to instruct children in the Puritan ethic.

51. Which of these examples of children's literature was not written in the eighteenth century?
    (Rigorous)

    A. Daniel Defoe's *Robinson Crusoe*

    B. Jonathan Swift's *Gulliver's Travels*

    C. John Newberry's *A Little Pretty Pocket-Book*

    D. Lewis Carroll's *Alice in Wonderland*

Answer: D. Lewis Carroll's *Alice in Wonderland*
Charles Lutwidge Dodgson, writing under the pen name Lewis Carroll, wrote *Alice in Wonderland* in 1865. *Gulliver's Travels* by Jonathan Swift was first published in 1726 and later amended in 1735. *Robinson Crusoe* by Daniel Defoe was first published in 1719 and is often considered the first English novel. *A Little Pretty Pocket-Book* by John Newberry was written in 1744 and sold with a ball for boys and a pincushion for girls. Also a publisher, John Newberry was recognized for his work in children's publishing by naming The Newberry Medal after him.

52. Which of the following characteristics identifies readers at the seventh and eighth grade reading levels?
    (Rigorous)

    A. Concern with establishing individual and peer group identities

    B. Strong perception of identity

    C. An awareness of ethics required by society

    D. Motivated by peer associations

Answer: A. Concern with establishing individual and peer group identities
Seventh and eighth graders are becoming concerned with establishing individual and peer group identities, which often presents conflicts with authority and the rigidity of rules. Some students at this age are still tied firmly to the family and its expectations, while others identify more with those their own age or older. Choices B, C, and D identify readers at the ninth grade level.

53. Which of these works would represent the concept of local color?
(Rigorous)

- A. "The Outcast of Poker Flats"
- B. "Daisy Miller: A Study"
- C. *Poems on Various Subjects*
- D. *Walden*

Answer: A. "The Outcast of Poker Flats"
Bret Harte's short story "The Outcast of Poker Flats" is a strong example of local color. Set in a California mining camp, the plot focuses on a group of ne'er do wells who are expelled by a group of vigilantes. Local color is defined as the presentation of the peculiarities of a particular locality and its inhabitants and is often marked by humor. The movement flourished after the Civil War, well after the publication of Thoreau's transcendental masterpiece *Walden*. Henry James' story "Daisy Miller: A Study" is an example of nineteenth-century social realism. Phyllis Wheatley's *Poems on Various Subjects* is a collection of poetry that is considered the first of African American literature.

54. Which period of literature emphasizes the individual, validates emotions and feelings, and looks to nature for inspiration?
(Easy)

- A. Neoclassicism
- B. Romanticism
- C. Realism
- D. Naturalism

Answer: B. Romanticism
Romantic literature emphasizes the individual. Emotions and feelings are validated, and nature acts as an inspiration for creativity. Patterned after the great writings of classical Greece and Rome, neoclassic literature is characterized by a balanced, graceful, well-crafted, refined, and elevated style. In neoclassical writing, the self is not exalted. Focus is on the group rather than the individual. Realistic writing deals with the common man and his socioeconomic problems in a non-sentimental way. Naturalism is realism pushed to its limit—writing that exposes the underbelly of society, usually the lower-class struggles.

55. Which of the following is not a member of the second generation of Romantic writers?
(Rigorous)

- A. John Keats
- B. Lord Byron
- C. Ralph Waldo Emerson
- D. Percy Bysshe Shelley

Answer: C. Ralph Waldo Emerson
Ralph Waldo Emerson is considered one of the first generation of Romantic writers (Wordsworth, Coleridge, Thoreau, Poe). Led by Wordsworth, this group maintained that the scenes and events of everyday life and the speech of ordinary people were the raw material from which poetry could and should be made. The second generation of Romantic writers (Keats, Byron, Shelley) stressed personal introspection and a love of beauty and nature as requisites for inspiration.

56. Which term can be defined as using all of one's experiences, learning, and development to comprehend information?
(Easy)

- A. Prior knowledge
- B. Context clues
- C. Comprehension
- D. Cues

Answer: A. Prior Knowledge
Prior knowledge is using all of one's prior experiences, learning, and development when entering a specific learning situation or attempting to comprehend a specific text. Sometimes prior knowledge can be erroneous or incomplete. Prior knowledge includes the accumulated positive and negative experiences that readers have acquired, both in and out of school. Context clues are words or sentences that help readers determine the meanings of words. Comprehension occurs when the reader correctly interprets the text and constructs meaning from it. Cues are used to direct and monitor reading comprehension.

57. In her journal, Gwenna writes an entry about reading *The Diary of Anne Frank*. Gwenna says that she understood how Anne felt about her mother since she had a fight with her own mother that morning before catching the school bus. What type of reading response does this represent?
(Average)

   A.   Critical

   B.   Emotional

   C.   Interpretive

   D.   Evaluative

Answer: B. Emotional
In an emotional response, readers can identify with the characters and situations so as to project themselves into the story. Critical responses involve making value judgments about the quality of a piece of literature. Interpretive responses lead to inferences about character development, setting, or plot; analysis of style elements; outcomes derivable from information provided in the narrative; and assessment of the author's intent. An evaluative response considers such factors as how well the piece of literature represents its genre, how well it reflects the social/ethical mores of society, and how well the author has approached the subject with regard to freshness and slant.

58. **Thom has explicated the Robert Frost poem "Mending Wall" in his final exam by analyzing the way the poem uses imagery and figures of speech to develop the theme of the poem. What type of literary response is this?** *(Average)*

    A. Emotional

    B. Interpretive

    C. Critical

    D. Evaluative

Answer: B. Interpretive
This is an example of an interpretive response, which lead to inferences about character development, setting, or plot; analysis of style elements; outcomes derivable from information provided in the narrative; and assessment of the author's intent. A critical response makes a value judgment about the quality of a piece of writing. In an emotional response, readers can identify with the characters and situations so as to project themselves into the story. An evaluative response considers such factors as how well the piece of literature represents its genre, how well it reflects the social/ethical mores of society, and how well the author has approached the subject with regard to freshness and slant.

59. **Mr. King has pulled together portfolios of students' work he has graded throughout the year. What is the correct term for this process?** *(Rigorous)*

    A. Evaluation

    B. Planning

    C. Assessment

    D. Interpretation

Answer: C. Assessment
The correct term is assessment, which is the practice of collecting information about students' progress. Evaluation is the process of judging the students' responses to determine how well they are achieving particular goals or demonstrating reading skills. Planning is formulating a plan of action. Interpretation is to explain the meaning of something.

60. **In Texas, students in the 10th grade participate in a series of tests called the Texas Assessment of Knowledge and Skills. What type of assessment is this?**
(Average)

    A. Formal

    B. Informal

    C. Holistic

    D. Summative

Answer: A. Formal
Formal assessment is composed of standardized tests and procedures carried out under prescribed conditions. Formal assessments include state tests, standardized achievement tests, NAEP tests, and the like. Informal assessment is the use of observation and other non-standardized procedures to compile anecdotal and observational data/evidence of children's progress. Informal assessment includes, but is not limited to, checklists, observations, and performance tasks. Holistic scoring is a method by which trained readers evaluate a piece of writing for its overall quality. Summative assessment summarizes the development of learners at a particular time.

61. **Which of these is not a skill to be evaluated when assessing reading comprehension?**
(Average)

    A. The ability to use schematic cues to connect words with prior knowledge

    B. The ability to use interpretive thinking to make logical predictions and inferences

    C. The ability to use secondary sources to clarify word meaning

    D. The ability to use appreciative thinking to respond to the text, whether emotionally, mentally, or ideologically

Answer: C. The ability to use secondary sources to clarify word meaning
There are a number of skills that can be evaluated to determine reading comprehension; however, the ability to use secondary sources, such as a dictionary, is not germane to the immediate reading process.

62. Which of the following is not correct?
(Rigorous)

- A. Good readers may substitute a word that does not fit the syntax, and will not correct themselves; poor readers will expect the word to fit the syntax they are familiar with

- B. Good readers will incorporate what they know with what the text says or implies; poor readers may think only of the word they are reading without associating it with prior knowledge

- C. Good readers will apply letter and sound associations almost subconsciously; poor readers may have undeveloped phonics skills or may use phonics skills in isolation

- D. Good readers will consider the meanings of all the known words in the sentence; poor readers may read one word at a time with no regard for the other words

Answer: A. Good readers may substitute a word that does not fit the syntax, and will not correct themselves; poor readers will expect the word to fit the syntax they are familiar with

Good readers will expect the word to fit the syntax they are familiar with. Poor readers may substitute a word that does not fit the syntax and will not correct themselves.

Directions: Read this poem and answer questions 63–66.

Piano

Softly, in the dusk, a woman is singing to me;
Taking me back down the vista of years, till I see
A child sitting under the piano, in the boom of the tingling strings
And pressing the small, poised feet of a mother who smiles as she sings.

In spite of myself, the insidious mastery of song
Betrays me back, till the heart of me weeps to belong
To the old Sunday evenings at home, with winter outside
And hymns in the cosy parlour, the tinkling piano our guide.

So now it is vain for the singer to burst into clamour
With the great black piano appassionato. The glamour
Of childish days is upon me, my manhood is cast
Down in the flood of remembrance, I weep like a child for the past.

—By D.H. Lawrence

63. What type of poetry is "Piano?
(Easy)

- A. Lyric
- B. Dramatic
- C. Narrative
- D. Epic

Answer: A. Lyric
"Piano" is a lyric poem because it is a short poem expressing the thoughts and feelings of a single speaker. It also has musical qualities, which was the original meaning of lyric poetry. A narrative poem tells a story. It has characters, setting, plot, and a narrative arc from exposition to denouement. Dramatic poetry presents the voice of a character speaking directly to the audience. It reveals key aspects of the character's psyche and sheds insight on the situation at hand. The audience takes the part of the silent listener, passing judgment and giving sympathy at the same time. In epic poetry, the action takes place in a social sphere rather than a personal sphere.

64. How can students determine the meaning of the word "insidious" used in line 5 of the poem?
(Average)

      A.   Context clues through word forms

      B.   Context clues through punctuation

      C.   Context clues through explanation

      D.   Context clues through sentence clues

Answer: D. Context clues through sentence clues
By reading this entire sentence (or stanza in this case), students can determine that "insidious" has a negative meaning, just like "betrays" and "weep." Even the phrase "in spite of myself" provides a clue that the "insidious" means working or spreading harmfully in a subtle or stealthy manner. There is no word form, punctuation, or explanation used to help determine the meaning.

65. How is connotation used to convey meaning in this poem?
(Average)

      A.   The words "insidious" and "betrays" convey the dark feelings of the poet

      B.   The end rhyme scheme mimics the beat of the piano

      C.   The repetition of the word "weep" adds impact

      D.   The musical term "appassionato" adds authenticity

Answer: A. The words "insidious" and "betrays" convey the dark feelings of the poet
Connotation is the emotional attachment that words convey. In this poem, the words "insidious" and "betrays" convey the dark feelings of the poet. While rhyme scheme can contribute to the tone of the poem, connotation relates to word choice. Repeating words may add impact but it is the meaning of the word that separates denotation from connotation. "Appassionato" is a musical term and, as used in this response, is meant to be considered in its denotative context.

66. **What would be an effective paraphrase of this poem?** *(Average)*

    A. "Piano" is a lyric poem reflecting the thoughts and feelings of a single speaker as he listens at dusk to a woman singing a song that brings back childhood memories of sitting at his mother's feet while she played the piano. It is a short poem of twelve lines divided into three quatrains, rhymed aabb. The poem contains vivid images, and specific and concrete details provide a clear embodiment of his memory.

    B. In the evening, a woman is singing for the speaker. This song takes him back to his childhood, and he sees a child sitting under the piano and listening to the sonorous music produced by the piano. In his childhood, his mother used to sit in a comfortable room and sing hymns. As a mischievous child, he used to press her legs but instead of showing her anger, she used to smile at him. When she sings the subtle song, it takes the speaker back to childhood, and his heart starts longing to be with the same piano at the cozy room of his house on Sunday evening. So, now it's vain for the singer to try to woo him and win his heart as the perfect figure of his mother is still in him, and he's driven back to childhood memories and is weeping like a child for the bygone days.

    C. The speaker in "Piano" by D. H. Lawrence is proud to be a full grown man, yet he loves remembering his happy childhood; his nostalgic attitude causes him to feel guilty as if he had betrayed his present state of being. Through effective imagery, Lawrence is able (to describe an image) to help the reader understand the speaker's nostalgic attitude. The diction and tone used in this poem reveal the speaker's struggle as his feelings mix between his desire to be a man and his desire to return to his childhood. The syntax and structure of the poem keep the reader in tune with the flow of the poem. In this poem, a man struggles to remain a man while fighting off his memories of the past, which he feels would be uncharacteristic of his present maturity.

    D. In a soft voice, a woman is singing to me. She is causing me to remember and look back through the years until I see in my imagination a child sitting under the piano among the noise of the playing strings and touching my mother's small poised feet while she is singing. Despite the fact that I am a man, I am seduced and song overcomes me—it brings me back through in a beguiling way until I weep in my heart to be a part of the old times on Sunday evenings at home when it is winter outside and where we all sat in the comfortable sitting room with the hymns sounding and with the sound of the piano keys as our guide. Now that those days are over, it is pointless for me to come and make a lot of noise along with a great piano piece that is full of passion. I am enveloped by the memories of the days of my childhood and I no longer am acting like a man, but instead I am weeping like a child because I long for the past.

Answer: D. In a soft voice, a woman is singing to me. She is causing me to remember and look back through the years until I see in my imagination a child sitting under the piano among the noise of the playing strings and touching my mother's small poised feet while she is singing. Despite the fact that I am a man, I am seduced and song overcomes me—it brings me back through in a beguiling way until I weep in my heart to be a part of the old times on Sunday evenings at home when it is winter outside and where we all sat in the comfortable sitting room with the hymns sounding and with the sound of the piano keys as our guide. Now that those day are over, it is pointless for me to come and make a lot of noise along with a great piano piece that is full of passion. I am enveloped by the memories of the days of my childhood and I no longer am acting like a man, but instead I am weeping like a child because I long for the past.

Paraphrasing is the art of rewording text. The goal is to maintain the original purpose of the statement while translating it into your own words. Choice D is an effective paraphrase. Choice A is a summary; it states the main idea and provides details about the poetic structure. Choice B is an unbalanced paraphrase by focusing on the beginning of the poem and neglecting the closing. Choice C is part summary, part critical analysis.

67. **Which of the following would not be an external factor affecting Juan's language development?**
    (Rigorous)

    A. Juan celebrates his 8th birthday

    B. Juan has emigrated from Puerto Rico and will begin 5th grade in an American school

    C. Juan is the youngest of four children

    D. Juan visits the library every week for story hour

Answer: A. Juan celebrates his 8th birthday
A child's age is an internal factor that affects language development. Immigration, birth order, and exposure to reading are all external factors.

68. Which approach of language development is based on the idea that children learn the rules of language structure and apply them through imitation and reinforcement?
    (Easy)

    A.   Learning approach

    B.   Linguistic approach

    C.   Cognitive approach

    D.   Sociocognitive approach

Answer: A. Learning approach
The learning approach believes that language develops from learning the rules of language structures and applying them through imitation and reinforcement. This approach also assumed that language, cognitive, and social developments were independent of each other. The linguistic approach believes that language ability is innate and develops through natural human maturation. The cognitive approach believes that language knowledge derives from syntactic and semantic structures. The sociocognitive approach believes that language development results from the interaction of language, cognitive, and social knowledge as part of the whole human development.

69. Which of the following would be the least effective way to incorporate the sociocognitive approach to learning development in a classroom?
    (Average)

    A.   Provide opportunities for students to make oral presentations

    B.   Encourage question-and-answer periods to stimulate discussion

    C.   Provide instruction on transformational grammar

    D.   Provide opportunities for group work

Answer: C. Provide instruction on transformational grammar
As a result of the sociocognitive approach in the 1970s, a larger emphasis has been placed on verbal communication. Thus, oral presentations, conversations, discussions, and group work encourage social interaction and enable speakers to apply their cognitive skills.

70. At what level does peer influence strongly affect language?
(Average)

    A.   Pre-school

    B.   Elementary school

    C.   Middle school

    D.   High school

Answer: C. Middle school
Once students begin school, their language is influenced by their peers although at the pre-school level, the prevailing influence is the home environment. During the elementary grades, students are influenced by interactions with their peers, but it is during the adolescence of the middle school years that this peer influence becomes more pronounced. Students at this age are becoming more independent of adult influence while developing their own sense of identity through association with their groups. This may continue or decrease in high school, depending on the students' maturity.

71. What is the history of a word called?
(Easy)

    A.   Vernacular

    B.   Neologism

    C.   Colloquialism

    D.   Etymology

Answer: A. Vernacular
The history of a word is called its etymology. Knowing the origins of a word can be very helpful in vocabulary study. A neologism is a new word or phrase added to the vocabulary. Recent neologisms include "twitter," "blogosphere," and "webinar." Technology and popular culture are two of the many driving forces that refresh our language. The language of a particular group of region in everyday conversation is called the vernacular. Similar to vernacular, a colloquialism is an informal word or phrase used by a particular group. Using contractions, for example, would be colloquial.

72. Which of the following is a not true about Old English?
(Average)

   A.   Introduced in Britain during the fifth century

   B.   Based on German language of the Angles, Saxons, and the Jutes

   C.   Used by Chaucer in *The Canterbury Tales*

   D.   Evolved from Indo-European languages through several hundreds of years

Answer: C. Used by Chaucer in *The Canterbury Tales*
Chaucer wrote in Middle English, which dates from 1066 when William the Conqueror invaded England. Prior to this Norman Conquest, Old English was the language introduced by German-speaking tribes in the fifth century. The German language is one of many languages spread out from Indo-European speakers several millenniums before.

73. Which of the following is a not true about Middle English?
(Average)

   A.   Developed in England after the Norman Conquest when William the Conqueror invaded from France

   B.   Used phonetic spelling and added more inflections

   C.   Used by Chaucer in *The Canterbury Tales*

   D.   Marked by the Great Vowel Shift when words like "maed" became "made"

Answer: D. Marked by the Great Vowel Shift when words like "maed" became "made"
The Great Vowel Shift in the 1500s is recognized as the beginning of Modern English. With the development of the printing press, language became standardized and vowels became differentiated between short and long. All of the other statements are true about Middle English.

74. Which of the following is not written in Middle English?
(Rigorous)

- A. Here begynneth a treatyse how yt hye
  fader of heuen sendeth dethe to so-
  mon euery creature to come and
  gyue counte of theyr liues in
  this worlde and is in maner
  of a morall playe.

- B. Upon an amblere esily she sat,
  Ywympled wel, and on hir heed an hat
  As brood as is a bokeler or a targe;
  A foot-mantel aboute hir hipes large,
  And on hir feet a paire of spores sharpe.

- C. Oft did she heave her napkin to her eyne,
  Which on it had conceited characters,
  Laund'ring the silken figures in the brine
  That seasoned woe had pelleted in tears,
  And often reading what contents it bears;
  As often shrieking undistinguished woe
  In clamours of all size, both high and low.

- D. HIt befel in the dayes of Vther pendragon when he was kynge of all Englond / and so regned that there was a myty duke in Cornewaill that helde warre ageynst hym long tyme.

**Answer: B. Upon an amblere esily she sat,
Ywympled wel, and on hir heed an hat
As brood as is a bokeler or a targe;
A foot-mantel aboute hir hipes large,
And on hir feet a paire of spores sharpe.**

Choice C is an excerpt from "A Lover's Complaint," a poem written by William Shakespeare in the sixteenth century during the Modern English period. Choice A is an excerpt from a morality play "Everyman" written in the late 1400s. Choice B is from the "The Wife of Bath's Prologue" by Geoffrey Chaucer, written at the end of the fourteenth century, which is the Middle English period. Choice D is an excerpt from "Le Morte D'Arthur," written by Sir Thomas Mallory in the 1400s.

75. Which of the following is true about Modern English?
(Rigorous)

   A.   Regional dialects remain a barrier to clear communication

   B.   The addition of new words has slowed since European immigration tapered off in the early 1900s

   C.   Technology has expanded English vocabulary

   D.   English is easier to learn because of its rules and structure

Answer: C. Technology has expanded English vocabulary
Because of technology, the English language is constantly growing; words like "google," "e-mail," and "blog" are some of the more ubiquitous neologisms. Radio, television, and movies have standardized pronunciation so dialects are no longer a barrier to communication. The language is in constant flux, so while European immigration may have slowed, new words continue to enter the language. In 2007 alone, Merriam-Webster added 100 new words to its dictionary. Although the rules of English give it structure, the exceptions to the rules complicate learning the language. While the language has lost many of its unnecessary inflections, it has borrowed words from other cultures and with these words come rules from the lender language.

76. Why are changes in syntax slow to occur in the English language?
(Rigorous)

   A.   The English language depends on word order to communicate meaning

   B.   The majority of English words has multiple meanings and can be used as different parts of speech

   C.   The English language depends heavily on inflections which affects syntax

   D.   Pronunciation and spelling make syntax changes more difficult

Answer: A. The English language depends on word order to communicate meaning
Because word order (syntax) communicates meaning, syntax is slow to change. Unlike other languages that depend on inflections, such as Spanish, the English language conveys ideas through the arrangement of words. Thus "Martina baked the cake" and "The cake baked Martina" have different meanings. Synonyms parts of speech, pronunciations, and spelling make English very flexible

77. Which of the following words does not have a bound morpheme?
(Rigorous)

    A.   Contract

    B.   Explanation

    C.   Dog

    D.   Words

Answer: D. Words
A bound morpheme is a linguistic unit that cannot stand alone. "Dog," a free morpheme, can stand alone. "Explanation" has a prefix "ex" and a suffix "ation." "Contractor" has a prefix "con" added to the base word "tract." "Words" has the suffix "-s" making the word plural.

78. In the word "conspirator," what does the prefix "con" mean?
(Rigorous)

    A.   Under

    B.   Not

    C.   With

    D.   Against

Answer: A. Under
The prefix "con" means "with." Understanding the meanings of prefixes can help students determine the meaning of unfamiliar words and realize that "conspirator," "conspire," and "conspiracy" have similar meanings. Knowing that "sub" means "under" can help students define "subterfuge." Knowing that "un" or "dis" means "not" can help students define "unconscionable" or "disingenuous." Knowing that "anti" means "against" can help students define "antidisestablishmentarianism"—although much more help and a dictionary are needed for that one.

79. Which of the following is true about spelling?
(Rigorous)

    A.   English spelling is based on the one-sound, one-letter formula

    B.   The English alphabet is based on the Greek alphabet with additions by the Romans

    C.   The English adopted the Latin-based alphabet with changes from the Greeks and Romans

    D.   English spelling became more erratic after the invention of the printing press

Answer: C. The English adopted the Latin-based alphabet with changes from the Greeks and Romans

The English alphabet is based on the Latin alphabet, which originally had twenty letters, consisting of the present English alphabet minus J, K, V, W, Y, and Z. The Romans added K to be used in abbreviations and Y and Z in words that came from the Greek. This 23-letter alphabet was adopted by the English, who developed W as a ligatured doubling of U and later J and V as consonantal variants of I and U. The result was our alphabet of 26 letters with upper case (capital) and lower case forms.

80. Which of the following is a simple sentence?
(Average)

    A.   Before doing their homework, they had to finish their chores; Megan set the table for dinner while Isaac peeled the potatoes.

    B.   After the class was over, the two students packed up their books and headed to the bus.

    C.   They talked and they laughed on their way home.

    D.   During 5th period English, Megan and Isaac opened their textbooks, turned to p. 35, and began to read the story in their reader.

Answer: D. During 5th period English, Megan and Isaac opened their textbooks, turned to p. 35, and began to read the story in their reader.
A simple sentence has one independent clause; an independent clause has one subject and verb combination. In choice D, the subject is compound (Megan, Isaac) and the verb is compound (opened, turned, read) but there is only one combination. Choice A is a compound-complex sentence: two independent clauses (they had/Megan set) joined by a semicolon and one dependent clause (while Isaac peeled). Choice B is a complex sentence; it begins a dependent clause (After the class was over) and ends with an independent clause (students, packed/headed). Choice C is a compound sentence with two independent clauses joined by a coordinating conjunction "and": (they talked/they laughed).

81. **Which sentence uses subordination to show cause and effect?**
    (Rigorous)

    A. After you review these terms, you should take the practice test.

    B. Although his insurance would have covered the fender bender, Harry decided to pay the garage himself.

    C. The non-profit reached its fundraising goal this year, which was surprising given the state of the economy.

    D. Because writers are seldom satisfied with their first drafts, they frequently revise and edit to craft a more precise message.

Answer: D. Because writers are seldom satisfied with their first drafts, they frequently revise and edit to craft a more precise message.
The subordinating conjunction "because" indicates cause and effect; in this example, the writers' dissatisfaction caused them to revise their messages. In choice A, the subordinating conjunction "after" indicates chronology or time order. In choice B, the subordinating conjunction "although" indicates contrast. In choice C, the subordinating conjunction "which" indicates condition.

82. **Which of the following sentences has a misplaced modifier?**
    (Rigorous)

    A. I showed my dog to the veterinarian with the fleas.

    B. Noxious fumes coming from the nearby plant made the office workers sick

    C. Feeling hot, the children took off their sweaters.

    D. The Honda was out of oil and stalled on the road.

Answer: A. I showed my dog to the veterinarian with the fleas.
Misplaced modifiers occur when phrases are not placed near the word they modify. In choice A, the dog should have the fleas, not the veterinarian. The sentence should be revised: I showed my dog with fleas to the veterinarian.

83. **Which of the following sentences has an error in parallel structure?**
    (Rigorous)

    A. During lunch, they were exchanging notes, studying for the test, and ate their sandwiches.

    B. The office is well-lit and air conditioned.

    C. Students attend class during the fall, winter, and spring, following a calendar that historically accommodated an agricultural society.

    D. As customers, we expect to be treated courteously and promptly.

Answer: A. During lunch, they were exchanging notes, studying for the test, and ate their sandwiches.
When a sentence contains a series of two or more related things or ideas, they should be expressed with a similar grammatical structure. In choice A, the three verb phrases are not parallel. The revised sentence should read "During lunch, they were exchanging notes, studying for the test, and eating their sandwiches." An alternative would be "During lunch, they exchanged notes, studied for the test, and ate their sandwiches.

84. **Choose the sentence with the correct subject-verb agreement.**
    (Average)

    A. Dewey, Cheatham, and Howe are the law firm that represents us.

    B. Neither the gym nor the cafeteria is open on the weekend.

    C. Either of the suggestions are acceptable.

    D. An important assignment, along with many resources, was misplaced.

Answer: B. Neither the gym nor the cafeteria is open on the weekend.
Subjects joined by "or" or "nor" may require singular or plural verbs. Make the verb agree with the closer subject. In choice B, "cafeteria" is singular so the verb should be "is." In choice A, the subject is a collective noun and takes a singular verb. In choice C, the indefinite pronoun "either" can be singular or plural; in this example, the word "suggestions" makes the verb plural. In choice D, a verb agrees with its subject regardless of intervening prepositional phrases or phrases introduced by "as well as," "in addition to," "such as," "including," "together with," and similar expressions.

85. Identify the sentence that is capitalized correctly.
    (Easy)

    A. The Gateway Arch in St. Louis is a memorial to Thomas Jefferson's role in opening the west, to the pioneers who helped shape its history, and to Dred Scott who sued for his freedom in the old courthouse.

    B. The Gateway arch in St. Louis is a memorial to Thomas Jefferson's role in opening the West, to the pioneers who helped shape its history, and to Dred Scott who sued for his freedom in the old Courthouse.

    C. The Gateway Arch in St. Louis is a memorial to Thomas Jefferson's role in opening the west, to the pioneers who helped shape its history, and to Dred Scott who sued for his freedom in the Old Courthouse.

    D. The Gateway Arch in St. Louis is a memorial to Thomas Jefferson's role in opening the West, to the pioneers who helped shape its history, and to Dred Scott who sued for his freedom in the Old Courthouse.

Answer: D. The Gateway Arch in St. Louis is a memorial to Thomas Jefferson's role in opening the West, to the pioneers who helped shape its history, and to Dred Scott who sued for his freedom in the Old Courthouse.
In choice D, capitalize proper nouns "Gateway Arch" and "Old Courthouse." Capitalize people's names such as "Thomas Jefferson" and "Dred Scott." Capitalize regions of the country such as "West."

86. Which process do most writers use to help them compose more efficiently and effectively?
    (Average)

    A. Step-by-step process

    B. Paraphrasing

    C. Documentation

    D. In-text citations

Answer: A. Step-by-step process
Writing is a recursive process in which students move back and forth as they move toward a finished product. By following a step-by-step process, they can compose more efficiently and effective. Paraphrasing is a form of summary in which a writer rephrases what someone else has written or said. Documentation establishes credibility by providing the source of evidence. An in-text citation is a form of documentation within the body of a paper.

87. **Which of the following is a common prewriting strategy?**
    (Easy)

    A. Keep an idea book; write in a daily journal

    B. Brainstorming

    C. Ask the questions who, what, where, when, and why, and how

    D. All of the above

Answer: D. All of the above
Using a number of different prewriting strategies will help students begin the writing process more effectively. All of these are effective. Others would include creating a visual map and using cluster circles and lines to show connection of ideas. If you can address the different learning styles of your students, you can provide them with a wide range of techniques to overcome the blank paper.

88. **What procedure should you follow during the writing stage?**
    (Average)

    A. Prepare an outline

    B. Make a list of all ideas connected with your topic

    C. Write freely

    D. Create a visual map on paper to gather ideas

Answer: C. Write freely
When students begin the writing stage, they should write freely, putting their ideas down on paper without stopping to edit or revise. Before they begin the writing stage, they would have made a list of ideas (prewriting/brainstorming), prepared an outline, and created a visual map to gather ideas.

89. In what stage of the writing process do writers make changes in sentences, wording, details, and ideas?
    (Average)

    A.　Prewriting

    B.　Writing

    C.　Revising

    D.　Publishing

Answer: C. Revising
In the revision stage, writers examine what they have written for unity, coherence, and development. They make changes in sentences, wording, details, and ideas so that their message is clear, complete, and concise. In the prewriting stage, writers gather ideas before writing. In the writing stage, writings compose the first draft, putting their ideas down freely. In the publishing stage, writers have their work displayed, printed, or distributed.

90. What is the goal of the publishing process?
    (Easy)

    A.　To have your work displayed on a bulletin board

    B.　To have your work read aloud in class

    C.　To have your work printed in a literary magazine or school anthology

    D.　All of the above

Answer: D. All of the above
Writing is hard work, and students should be encouraged to share the works of their labor. Using a variety of traditional and electronic publishing means, student writers can celebrate their achievements, share their ideas, and learn from each other.

91. Which of these errors would be caught by a spellchecker?
(Average)

- A. Alice went threw the looking glass.

- B. The pep squad won't not be participating.

- C. I attended seminar about effective teaching techniques.

- D. The coach announced the the starting line-up.

Answer: D. The coach announced the the starting line-up.
Computer spellcheckers will catch when a word is repeated as in "The Coach announced the the starting line-up." However, they will not catch homonyms as in misusing threw for through. They will not catch poor grammar as in the double negative "won't not." They will not catch missing words as in "I attended a seminar..."

92. Mr. McCutcheon is helping students write their first draft of an argumentative essay and notes that many students are having a hard time with pronoun-antecedent agreement. What would be an effective teaching strategy?
(Rigorous)

- A. Develop a three-day grammar workshop to address mechanical problems.

- B. Stop the class and provide a brief explanation of the problem and ways to correct.

- C. Assign a homework exercise in which students correct sentences with pronoun-antecedent errors.

- D. Distribute grammar textbooks and tell students to review the section on pronoun use.

Answer: B. Stop the class and provide a brief explanation of the problem and ways to correct.
During the writing process, grammar instruction should be provided within the context of the assignment. This scenario is an example of a "teachable moment." Mr. McCutcheon should stop the class and, using examples from the students' writings, provide a brief explanation of the problem and ways to correct. While the other strategies have value, grammar does not have to be taught in isolation, as in a three-day workshop. Even though practice is valuable, students would not welcome a homework assignment nor would they necessarily be able to understand and correct this error independently.

93. **When assessing and responding to student writing, which guideline is not summative?**
    (Rigorous)

    A.   Reread the writing and note at the end whether the student met the objective of the writing task

    B.   Ask students to submit prewriting and rough-draft materials, including all revisions, with their final draft

    C.   When reading the draft for the second time, assess it using the standards previously established

    D.   Make sure you address the process as well as the product. It is important that students value the learning process as well as the final product

Answer: A. Reread the writing and note at the end whether the student met the objective of the writing task

Summative assessment is the collection of data to measure the product of learning. It includes observations, performance work, unit project work, portfolio assessments, self-assessments, and additional selected assessment instruments and rubrics. Formative assessment is ongoing assessment used to determine how well students are working toward an objective or expectation. It includes the use of checklists, conferences, self-assessment, and focused observation. Choice A "Reread the writing and note at the end whether the student met the objective of the writing task" is formative.

94. **Which of the following suggestions are used for Integrating Language Arts?**
    (Average)

    A. Create writing activities that are relevant to students by having them write and share with real audiences

    B. Use pre-reading activities such as discussion, writing, research, and journals

    C. Use prewriting activities such as reading model essays, researching a topic, interviewing others, and combining sentences

    D. All of the above

Answer: D. All of the above
All of the above are effective ways to integrate language arts. Also called "language across the curriculum," this is a method to provide natural learning situations in all aspects of learning. Reading, writing, speaking, listening, and viewing enables students to make connections between each aspect of language development during every class.

95. **What is not an effective step that students should follow when gathering data or information?**
    (Average)

    A. Keep a record of any sources consulted during the research process

    B. Use only direct quotes to avoid plagiarism

    C. Summarize and paraphrase in their own words without the source in front of them

    D. Use key words and synonyms to search for information

Answer: B. Use only direct quotes to avoid plagiarism
Research can be an overwhelming process, but it can be made easier if students are taught good habits in gathering data. By keeping a record of sources, they will be able to document their information correctly. While direct quotes can be effective to make a point, they should be used judiciously and sparingly. Instead, as they take notes, they should put the information in their own words by either summarizing or paraphrasing.

96. **When searching online databases for information about the effects of global warming on the polar ice caps, which Boolean operators will generate the highest number of hits?**
    (Rigorous)

    A.   "global warming" and "polar ice caps"

    B.   "global warming" not "polar ice caps"

    C.   "global warming" or "polar ice caps"

    D.   (global warming) and (polar ice caps)

Answer: C. "global warming" or "polar ice caps"
By using "or" the search is broadened and will retrieve records containing any of the words the operator separates: global, warming, polar, ice caps. By using "and," the search is narrowed and will retrieve records containing all of the words the operator separates. By using "not," the search is narrowed and will retrieve records for only the first term (global warming) and not for the second term (polar ice caps). Using the parenthesis to group words and phrases will show the order in which the relationship should be considered, such as (global or warming) and (polar or ice cap).

97. **What are the two major groups of research materials?**
    (Easy)

    A.   Primary and secondary

    B.   Hard copy and electronic

    C.   Library and online

    D.   Informational and analytical

Answer: A. Primary and secondary
The two major groups of research materials are primary and secondary. Primary sources are works, records, and the like that were created during the period being studied, such as archeological artifacts or diaries. Primary sources are the basic materials that provide the raw data and information. Secondary sources are works written after the period being studied and explain the primary sources. For example, the novel *Jane Eyre* would be a primary source but a collection of literary critiques about *Jane Eyre* would be a secondary source.

98. Which of following materials are secondary sources?
(Rigorous)

   A.   Books written on the basis of primary materials about the period of time

   B.   Books written on the basis of primary materials about persons who played a major role in the events under consideration

   C.   Books and articles written on the basis of primary materials about the culture, the social norms, the language, and the values of the period

   D.   All of the above

Answer: D. All of the above
Primary sources are works, records, and the like that were created during the period being studied, such as archeological artifacts or diaries. Primary sources are the basic materials that provide the raw data and information. Secondary sources are works written after the period being studied and explain the primary sources. For example, the novel *Jane Eyre* would be a primary source but a collection of literary critiques about *Jane Eyre* would be a secondary source.

99. Martin is writing a research paper about the role of African Americans in the Vietnam War. Which of these would be an example of primary research?
(Rigorous)

   A.   Martin reads *Soul Soldiers* by Richard Bailey

   B.   Martin finds three online articles about the roles of minorities in the Vietnam War

   C.   Martin interviews his grandfather, who served two tours in Vietnam as a medic

   D.   Martin finds information on the website www.blackmilitaryworld.com

Answer: C. Martin interviews his grandfather, who served two tours in Vietnam as a medic
An interview is a primary method of gathering information. By interviewing his grandfather, Martin is getting a first-hand account of information. The book, articles, and website are secondary sources, based on data gathered by the others.

100. **Which of the following is not an appropriate way to paraphrase correctly?**
    (Average)

    A.   Change concept words, special terms, or proper names

    B.   Change the key words' form or part of speech

    C.   Use synonyms of "relationship words," and use synonyms of phrases and words

    D.   Change passive voice to active voice or move phrases and modifiers

Answer: A. Change concept words, special terms, or proper names
Paraphrasing is the art of rewording text. The goal is to maintain the original purpose of the statement while translating it into your own words. Your newly generated sentence can be longer or shorter than the original. Concentrate on the meaning, not on the words. Do not change concept words, special terms, or proper names.

101. **Hermione is looking for scholarly information on building an environmentally friendly house. Based on domain names, which site is the most likely to be useful?**
    (Easy)

    A.   Wikipedia.com

    B.   USA.gov

    C.   Greenpeople.org

    D.   Healthybuilding.net

Answer: B. USA.gov
Domain names are just one way to determine the credibility of information. Sites with the ".gov" domain name are hosted by the government and are considered trustworthy. The "com" domain is used by for-profit business sites. The "org" domain is used by non-profit organizations and professional associations. The "net" domain is used by organizations in network access. All of these sites may indeed have useful and credible information and researchers must continually evaluate their information.

102. What are some the consequences students should be aware of in violating the rules applying to borrowing ideas from various sources?
(Average)

    A.   Failing an assignment

    B.   Expulsion and civil penalties

    C.   Losing credit for an entire course

    D.   All of the above

Answer: D. All of the above
Documentation is an important skill when incorporating outside information into a piece of writing. Students must learn that research involves more than cutting and pasting from the Internet and that plagiarism is a serious academic offense, punishable in a number of ways.

103. Which of the following is the correct example of MLA in-text citation?
(Rigorous)

    A.   Hu believes that beginning math teachers enter the classroom with a minimal knowledge of math (Hu 2).

    B.   Hu believes that beginning math teachers enter the classroom with a minimal knowledge of math (2).

    C.   Hu believes that beginning math teachers enter the classroom with a minimal knowledge of math (Hu, 2000).

    D.   Hu (2000) believes that beginning math teachers enter the classroom with a minimal knowledge of math (2).

Answer: B. Hu believes that beginning math teachers enter the classroom with a minimal knowledge of math (2).
According to the MLA style, the author's name and page number are placed in parentheses at the end of a sentence; if the author's name is in the sentence, then only the page number is put in parentheses.

104. What are the two characteristics that determine language style?
(Rigorous)

   A. Degree of formality and word choice

   B. Formal writing and informal writing

   C. Tone and writer's attitude

   D. Point of view and substance

Answer: A. Degree of formality and word choice
Two characteristics that determine language style are degree of formality and word choice. The most formal language does not use contractions or slang, while the most informal language will probably feature a more casual use of common sayings and anecdotes. Formal language uses longer sentences and does not sound like a conversation. Informal language uses shorter sentences (not necessarily simple sentences, but shorter constructions) and may sound like a conversation.

105. Which of the following does not exist in formal language?
(Rigorous)

   A. Uses shorter sentences and may sound like a conversation

   B. Does not use contractions or slang

   C. Tone—writer's attitude toward the material and/or reader

   D. Uses longer sentences and does not sound like a conversation

Answer: A. Uses shorter sentences and may sound like a conversation
Two characteristics that determine language style are degree of formality and word choice. The most formal language does not use contractions or slang, while the most informal language will probably feature a more casual use of common sayings and anecdotes. Formal language uses longer sentences and does not sound like a conversation. Informal language uses shorter sentences (not necessarily simple sentences, but shorter constructions) and may sound like a conversation.

106. Which of the following is not a suggestion that will help students to be more meaningful engaged in their writing?
(Rigorous)

   A.   Write for the teacher as the audience

   B.   Write stories that could be read aloud to a group or published in a literary magazine or class anthology

   C.   Write for different audiences

   D.   Write for different purposes

Answer: A. Write for the teacher as the audience
In the past, teachers have assigned reports, paragraphs, and essays that focused on the teacher as the audience. The purpose of the writing was to explain information. However, for students to be meaningfully engaged in their writing, they must write for a variety of reasons. Writing for different audiences and aims encourages students to be more involved. If they write for the same audience and purpose, they will continue to see writing as just another assignment.

107. Allyson is preparing a report for the school's English department to recommend a new course for seniors. She determines that of the ten readers, six are women and four are men; eight have bachelor's degrees, one has a master's degree, and one has a doctoral degree. Which of the following has she assessed about her audience?
(Easy)

   A.   Values

   B.   Needs

   C.   Constraints

   D.   Demographics

Answer: A. Values
Writers will want to assess their audience so they can tailor their writing to achieve their purpose. By assessing demographics, Allyson is identifying the quantifiable characteristics, such as age, gender, and education. In assessing the values, writers are determining the beliefs of the readers. By assessing needs, writers are identifying what the audience requires. By assessing constraints, writers are identifying limitations.

108. To be convincing, in writing or speaking, which of the following is not one of the three basic principles to follow?
(Average)

- A. Transition
- B. Coherence
- C. Unity
- D. Emphasis

Answer: A. Transition
In writing or speaking, you can be convincing if you follow the three basic principles of unity, coherence, and emphasis. To achieve unity, all ideas must relate to the controlling thesis. To achieve coherence, use transitional words, phrases, sentences, and paragraphs to show relationship of ideas. To achieve emphasis, arrange ideas in strategic order to show their significance.

109. What is the structural problem with this paragraph?
(Average)

Club Palm Resort's beaches are beautiful, and the surrounding countryside is quite scenic. The quality of the food leaves a lot to be desired. Many vacationers enjoy the variety of outdoor activities and the instruction available in such sports as sailing and scuba diving. Unfortunately, security is poor; several vacationers' rooms have been broken into and their valuables stolen. Christmas in the Bahamas can make the thought of New Year's in Chicago bearable.

- A. Development
- B. Coherence
- C. Unity
- D. Transition

Answer: C. Unity
This paragraph lacks unity. It jumps from one idea to another (scenery, food, sports, security) without any controlling idea to hold them together. One way to achieve unity is to write a topic sentence that holds all these together. Another would be to use transitional words or phrases to show the relationship of ideas.

110. What is a disadvantage of a print message?
(Easy)

- A. A print message has longevity and is easily portable
- B. A print message requires a skillful reader
- C. A print message appeals to the mind
- D. A print message enables students to re-read sections

Answer: B. A print message requires a skillful reader

A print message has both positive and negative features. For instance, print messages have longevity; they are also easily portable. Print messages appeal almost exclusively to the mind and allow students to recursively read sections that warrant more thought. On the negative side, a print message requires a skillful reader; without such a reader, print messages are not very effective. Print messages are not accessible to non-readers.

111. Which message offers the easiest accessibility for learners?
(Average)

- A. Print
- B. Audio
- C. Multimedia
- D. Audiovisual

Answer: D. Audiovisual

An audiovisual message offers the easiest accessibility for learners. It has the advantages of both the graphic and the audio medium. Learners' eyes and ears are engaged. Non-readers get significant access to content.

112. What type of written discourse gives information not previously known about a topic or is used to explain or define a topic?
(Average)

    A.   Narrative writing

    B.   Descriptive writing

    C.   Persuasive writing

    D.   Basic expository writing

Answer: D. Basic expository writing
Basic expository writing simply gives information not previously known about a topic or is used to explain or define a topic. Facts, examples, statistics, and non-emotional information are presented in a formal manner. The tone is direct and the delivery objective rather than subjective. Descriptive writing centers on person, place, or object, using sensory words to create a mood or impression and arranging details in a chronological or spatial sequence. Persuasive writing implies the writer's ability to select vocabulary and arrange facts and opinions in such a way as to direct the actions of the listener/reader. Persuasive writing may incorporate exposition and narration as they illustrate the main idea. Narrative writing is developed using an incident or anecdote or a related series of events. Chronology, the 5 Ws, topic sentence, and conclusion are essential ingredients.

113. Which of the following provides opportunities for students to apply expository and informative communication?
(Rigorous)

    A.   Speeches

    B.   Interviewing

    C.   Memorization

    D.   Recitation

Answer: B. Interviewing
Interviewing provides opportunities for students to apply expository and informative communication by teaching them how to structure questions to evoke fact-filled responses. Compiling the information from an interview into a biographical essay or speech helps students list, sort, and arrange details in an orderly fashion.

114. Which of the following would not be an effective delivery technique for oral presentations?
(Easy)

- A. Maintain a straight but not stiff posture
- B. Refrain from using gestures
- C. Stay within four to eight feet of the front row of your audience
- D. Vary the tone of your voice to show emphasis

Answer: B. Refrain from using gestures
Gestures can help a speaker maintain a natural atmosphere when speaking publicly; however, they shouldn't be exaggerated or distracting. Gestures can be used for added emphasis.

115. What uses the idea that facts, statistics, and other forms of evidence can convince an audience to accept a speaker's argument?
(Rigorous)

- A. Ethos
- B. Pathos
- C. Culture
- D. Logos

Answer: D. Logos
Logos refers to the logic of the speaker's argument. It uses the idea that facts, statistics, and other forms of evidence can convince an audience to accept a speaker's argument. Pathos refers to the emotional appeal made by the speaker to the listener. It emphasizes the fact that an audience responds to ideas with emotion. Ethos refers to the credibility of the speaker. It establishes the speaker as a reliable and trustworthy authority by focusing on the speaker's credentials. Culture is a shared system of beliefs, attitudes, values, and dispositions.

116. Which of the following is not a form of inductive reasoning?
(Average)

   A.   Reasoning that goes from general observations to a particular conclusion

   B.   Reasoning that goes from particular observations to a general conclusion

   C.   Reasoning from a specific case or cases and deriving a general rule

   D.   Reasoning that draws inferences from observations in order to make generalizations

Answer: A. Reasoning that goes from general observations to a particular conclusion
The two forms of reasoning used to support an argument are inductive and deductive. Inductive reasoning goes from particular observations to a general conclusion. Deductive reasoning, on the other hand, reverses the order by going from general to particular.

117. Which of the following is an example of deductive logic?
(Rigorous)

   A.   All men are mortal; Joe is a man; therefore Joe is mortal

   B.   Bachelors are unmarried men; Bill is unmarried; therefore, Bill is a bachelor

   C.   A professional basketball game has four periods; we attended a pro basketball game; wherefore it had four periods

   D.   This cat is black; that cat is black; a third cat is black; therefore all cats are black

Answer: D. This cat is black; that cat is black A third cat is black; therefore all cats are black
Deductive reasoning is one of the two basic forms of valid reasoning. While inductive reasoning argues from the particular to the general, deductive reasoning argues from the general to a specific instance. The basic idea is that if something is true of a class of things in general, this truth applies to all legitimate members of that class. The key, then, is to be able to properly identify members of the class. In choice D, the argument is moving from the specific to a general conclusion.

118. What form of persuasive speech appeals to both reason and emotion, and tells listeners what they can do and how to do it?
(Rigorous)

    A.   Policy

    B.   Value

    C.   Fact

    D.   Argumentation

Answer: A. Policy
Policy is the type of speech that is a call to action, arguing that something should be done, improved, or changed. Its goal is action from the audience, but it also seeks passive agreement with the proposition proposed. It appeals to both reason and emotion and tells listeners what they can do and how to do it. Value tries to convince the audience that a certain thing is good or bad, moral or immoral, valuable or worthless. It focuses less on knowledge and more on beliefs and values. Fact tries to find an answer based on the evidence provided. Argumentation is synonym for persuasion, although a distinction is often made that argumentation appeals to reason while persuasion appeals to emotion.

119. **Which of the following describes third-person omniscient?**
    (Easy)

    A. The narrator is not seen or acting in the story but is able to watch and record not only what is happening or being said but also what characters are thinking

    B. Narrator participates in action but sometimes has limited knowledge/vision

    C. The narrator is all-knowing about one or two characters but not all of them

    D. The narrator talks to the reader and, in essence, draws the reader into the story

Answer: A. The narrator is not seen or acting in the story but is able to watch and record not only what is happening or being said but also what characters are thinking
Point of view or voice is the character through which the reader sees the action. The most common of the many points of view is third-person omniscient: the narrator is all-knowing and relates what others can see, think, and feel. Choice B is first-person limited point of view. Choice C is third-person limited omniscient. Choice D is second-person point of view, which is rarely used. An example would be Jay McInerney's *Bright Lights, Big City*.

120. **In a job interview, Colleen, a recent graduate, explains how proud she is that she worked twenty hours a week while attending college and still maintained a 3.2 GPA. She voices her disdain about other graduates who had no outside jobs and earned lower GPAs. Which form of bias is seen in this example?**
    (Rigorous)

    A. Cultural bias

    B. Racial bias

    C. Professional bias

    D. Unconscious bias

Answer: A. Cultural bias
Culture is a shared system of beliefs, attitudes and values. In this example, Colleen has shown that she values her ability to achieve more than others who had fewer limitations.

Answer Key

1.	C	41.	A	81.	D
2.	A	42.	C	82.	A
3.	C	43.	C	83.	A
4.	D	44.	D	84.	B
5.	D	45.	D	85.	D
6.	B	46.	C	86.	A
7.	B	47.	D	87.	D
8.	B	48.	D	88.	C
9.	A	49.	A	89.	C
10.	C	50.	A	90.	D
11.	C	51.	D	91.	D
12.	D	52.	A	92.	B
13.	A	53.	A	93.	A
14.	C	54.	B	94.	D
15.	D	55.	C	95.	B
16.	C	56.	A	96.	C
17.	C	57.	B	97.	A
18.	B	58.	B	98.	D
19.	D	59.	C	99.	C
20.	C	60.	A	100.	A
21.	A	61.	C	101.	B
22.	D	62.	A	102.	D
23.	B	63.	A	103.	B
24.	D	64.	D	104.	A
25.	C	65.	A	105.	A
26.	A	66.	D	106.	A
27.	B	67.	A	107.	A
28.	C	68.	A	108.	A
29.	A	69.	C	109.	C
30.	B	70.	C	110.	B
31.	A	71.	A	111.	D
32.	B	72.	C	112.	D
33.	D	73.	D	113.	B
34.	A	74.	B	114.	B
35.	C	75.	C	115.	D
36.	D	76.	A	116.	A
37.	A	77.	D	117.	D
38.	D	78.	A	118.	A
39.	A	79.	C	119.	A
40.	B	80.	D	120.	A

Rigor Table

	Easy 20%	Average 40%	Rigorous 40%
Questions	2, 4, 13, 17, 18, 20, 23, 25, 31, 38, 54, 56, 63, 68, 71, 85, 87, 90, 97, 101, 107, 110, 114, 119	5, 6, 7, 12, 16, 19, 21, 22, 24, 26, 27, 32, 33, 35, 36, 37, 40, 42, 46, 47, 48, 49, 57, 58, 60, 61, 64, 65, 66, 69, 70, 72, 73, 80, 84, 86, 88, 89, 91, 94, 95, 100, 102, 108, 109, 111, 112, 116	1, 3, 8, 9, 10, 11, 14, 15, 28, 29, 30, 34, 39, 41, 43, 44, 45, 50, 51, 52, 53, 55, 59, 62, 67, 74, 75, 76, 77, 78, 79, 81, 82, 83, 92, 93, 96, 98, 99, 103, 104, 105, 106, 113, 115, 117, 118, 120

www.ingramcontent.com/pod-product-compliance
Lightning Source LLC
LaVergne TN
LVHW061313060426
835507LV00019B/2136